William
Carey

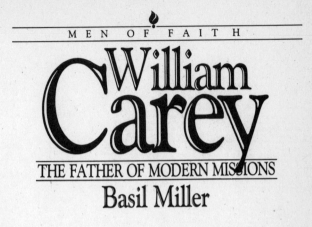

MEN OF FAITH

William Carey

THE FATHER OF MODERN MISSIONS

Basil Miller

BETHANY HOUSE PUBLISHERS
MINNEAPOLIS, MINNESOTA 55438
A Division of Bethany Fellowship, Inc.

William Carey: The Father of Modern Missions
Basil Miller

Library of Congress Catalog Card Number 85-71476

ISBN 0-87123-850-0

Published by Bethany House Publishers
A Division of Bethany Fellowship, Inc.
6820 Auto Club Road, Minneapolis, Minnesota 55438

Printed in the United States of America

CONTENTS

Chapter 1

THE AWAKENING LAD

WILLIAM CAREY sired the modern missionary movement. The dream of worldwide missions flamed forth first in his mind and soul, and through the generations since his time this idea has become a living reality. Few names in the annals of the Church sound with greater glory than his.

There was little in Carey's background to indicate the greatness that was to stem from his life. His career points to the fact that God in the life of man can achieve the impossible. There was no promise of genius in his youth, yet before he died he laid upon the Christian world a debt of eternal gratitude. From a poor English lad with little education, he became a noted Sanskrit scholar and changed the outlook of an empire.

As incredible as it seems, though practically untutored, Carey gave the Bible to more of the earth's inhabitants than any other man. His life, once God touched and enobled it, flashed forth spiritual beauty from many unsuspected facets.

There was an ever-expanding desire for service in his soul that would not be satisfied once God had given him the vision. William Carey as a lad literally hitched the wagon of his life to the Star of Bethlehem, and it was his faith in, and his reliance upon, God that led him from the cobbler's bench to a position of renown in the annals of Missionary history.

Carey never claimed personal credit for his achievements. The supreme thought underlying all his actions was, "What hath God wrought?"

By aligning his life with the laws of divine leadership, Carey climbed to the heights of spiritual achievement. Millions have been blessed by the results of his consecration and complete surrender to the divine will. Yielding himself confidently to the Master, Carey marched forward to wondrous accomplishments for God and missions.

Practically untaught, he became learned. Poor himself, he made millions spiritually rich. By birth obscure he scaled the heights of eminence, seeking only to follow the Lord's leadership, inspired by the forward march of God's plans.

It was he who put wheels to the divine vision of evangelizing the world. While others were content to let the heathen stream over the brink of eternity unreached and un-evangelized, William Carey proclaimed that the Gospel must be heralded to the ends of the world, willing to lay his life upon the altar of martyrdom if need be to bring this dream to fruition and living reality.

God drew back the curtains of eternity and showed Carey the vision of the heathen rejoicing in the knowledge of salvation. Carey in turn yielded his life in complete surrender to the divine unction and walked forth in humble faith to be one of the first to carry the glad story to those that sat in heathen darkness. He began a movement which will know no end until the kingdoms of this world shall become the kingdoms of our God.

Carey was born August 17, 1761, at Paulerspury, a small village in the southeast corner of Northamptonshire, some ten miles from the town of Northampton. The region was rich in historical and literary tradition, though these little touched the Carey home at the time. The battle of Naseby had been fought near Carey's home. From the same section had come the founders of Harvard College. Here also lived the forebears of George Washington and Benjamin Franklin. Other illustrious sons from this same area included William Law, author of the famous book, *The Serious Call*, John Gill, the scholar, Phillip Doddridge, James Kirby and other noted preachers and religious workers.

The rolling and wooded countryside appealed to Carey's nature-loving spirit. Handicrafts flourished in the many little villages. William's father, Edmund Carey, was a weaver of a cloth known as "tammy cloth," a popular fabric at the time. Six years after William's birth the father became a schoolmaster and parish clerk, at which time the family moved from their humble cottage to the teacher's home belonging to the free school at the church end of the village. William's grandfather, Peter Carey, who had come to Paulerspury in his early manhood, had filled the same office. The Carey family must have stood high in village esteem.

The Careys had lived in Paulerspury and at Olney, some ten miles distant, for a hundred years or more. One Carey, from 1624 to 1629, had been a curate in the district and wrote what was called, "a tolerable hand." There were two branches of the family, one definitely poor, and the other sufficiently well off "to be buried in woolens." The poorer members were interred "in a coffin only." The lack of a shroud spelled poverty. William's family, by the time of the lad's arrival, could have qualified for either. They were poor enough to belong to the shroudless class, but with father Edmund a schoolteacher, this raised the financial status of the family from the "coffin only" to the "buried in woolens" group.

The village was blessed with an endowed school. One of the chief citizens, William Marriot, had left what amounted to $30.00 a year "towards the schooling of six boys in the village." A London citizen with lands near Pury

followed Marriot's example. So before national schools
were known and while village charity schools were rare,
Pury had a dozen free scholarships for the boys.

The Careys, though poor, were learned, for William's
grandfather, Peter Carey, became the first schoolmaster and
also parish clerk. A specimen of his handwriting, which
is still extant and is described as free and elegant, indi-
cates that Grandfather Carey was no mere rustic. His
oldest son likewise followed his footsteps and became a
teacher in the nearby town of Lowcester, though he died
at the early age of twenty. Grandfather Peter was so
stricken that he followed his son to the grave in two weeks,
leaving his widow, Ann, and Edmund, then but a boy, to
fend for themselves.

Another son of Grandfather Carey had gone to Canada
and disappeared as far as the rest of the family was concerned. Edmund was given one of the free school scholarships by his village. He learned easily and devoted himself
to the support of his mother. When he was twenty-four he
married Elizabeth Wells, and Grandmother Carey henceforth made her home with Edmund and Elizabeth.

Their first child was named William. The new baby
became the grandmother's special care. She was a sweet,
gentle and religious person, and her loving attentions
and constant association with him made a lasting impression
upon the boy's youthful growing nature.

The house to which the family moved when William was
six was an improvement over the tiny cottage in which he
was born. In front, two wide-spreading trees gave grace
and beauty to the building. At the rear stretched a
garden and orchard. A nearby moat afforded a glorious
fishing place for the lad. Not far away ran a coach road
from London to Chester. As the coaches swept by, the boy's
imagination was often stirred to wondering about the far-
off places dotting that rambling road.

The Royal Forest, with its low hills and gentle valleys, was near at hand, inviting the boy to wander within its confines. He learned to investigate and ponder upon the life of plants and animals which he found there. Young William enjoyed all this immensely, his innate love of nature causing him to delight in the beautiful wild life abounding in the place.

In his new home William had a room of his own. This soon took on all the aspects of a baby natural history museum. Here young William impounded insects, birds, bird eggs, botanical specimens, anything and everything that attracted his attention during his tours through the lanes and meadows and the Royal Whittlebury Forest. With a collector's instinct he gathered specimens from far and wide. When a mere boy, he became known for his knowledge of natural history. When a query arose about some flower, insect or bird, William's counsel or advice was sought by the villagers.

"Take it to Bill Carey. He'll tell you all about it," said his acquaintances when an object of interest was discovered.

"Of birds, and all manner of insects, he had numbers," wrote his sister Mary of the boy's growing collection. "When he was away from home the birds were committed to my care. Since I was more than five years younger, he showered me with all his enjoyments. Though often I killed his pets with kindness, yet when he saw my grief over them, he always relented and gave me the pleasure of serving them again. He often took me over the dirtiest roads to get at a plant or an insect. He never walked out . . . without making observations on the hedge as he passed, and when he took up a plant of any kind he studied it with care."

As soon as he was old enough William took charge of his father's garden, and it became the show spot of the village.

Three more children had been born into the family by this time: Ann, who was named for her grandmother, Mary Elizabeth, who died in her infancy, and a brother, Thomas. The children went to school and were instructed by their father.

"Our father permitted," said Mary, speaking of their school days, "no partiality for the abilities of his own children, but rather went too far the other way sometimes, which tended to discourage them a little."

William had a natural thirst for knowledge. A constant urge drove his mind into the nooks and crannies where information was to be found. He read all the books the school afforded. When he was not reading he was tramping the fields, trying to discover the secrets of nature. It was natural for him to center his attention solidly upon any object he might be studying at the moment.

There was not a lazy fiber in William's mental mechanism. His sister said of him, "Whatever he began he finished. Difficulties never discouraged him."

"From a boy he was studious," said William's brother Thomas, "deeply bent on learning all he could and determined not to give up a particle of anything on which his mind was set, until he had arrived at a clear knowledge and sense of the subject. He was neither diverted by allurements, nor driven from his search by ridicule or threats."

These characteristics marked the life of William Carey and qualified him to become one of the leading scholars of his generation. In later years he called himself a "plodder" and said that he could persevere to all limits in any definite pursuit. He loved to do a task thoroughly, whatever its nature, and desired to complete a study once it was undertaken. As a growing schoolboy, he learned to compile information upon any subject he was studying to such an extent that it satisfied even his own critical demands. He was apt in arithmetic. His mother often heard him "cashing accounts" at night, after all the family had retired.

Books were scarce even in a schoolmaster's home. Those within the family William read and reread. When he had finished these time and again, he borrowed as extensively as possible. Whenever he could lay his hand upon a book, his eager mind soon devoured the contents.

"I chose to read books of science, history and voyages, more than any others," said the mature William, looking back on his childhood. "Novels and plays always disgusted me. I avoided them as much as I did books on religion. I was better pleased with romances, and this prompted me to read the *Pilgrim's Progress* with eagerness but without purpose."

William was enchanted with the story of Columbus. He talked so much of this famous explorer that he was nicknamed Columbus by his companions. The boys of the village often said to him, "Well if you won't play, preach us a sermon." And William would mount an old stump and hold forth on the deeds and persistence and accomplishments of the discoverer of the New World.

Doubtless this interest was abetted by the return of his long-lost Uncle Peter from Canada. Uncle Peter who had the knack of wrapping up his own life with stories of adventure in the wilds of Canada, told many interesting things about the land beyond the sea. His uncle shared William's love for plants and their culture and he became a gardener on a neighboring estate. Thus uncle and nephew with mutual interest in voyaging and voyages, and in the care and development of growing things, became boon companions.

William's religious life was not overlooked, though at the time it influenced the lad only slightly. He was neither conspicuously unruly as a boy, nor noticeably religious. He regularly attended the church as a member of a church-going family naturally would. For a time he sang in the boys' choir. He became familiar with the Bible, the catechism and the Prayer Book. His devout grandmother taught him much about the deeper meanings of religious living, and both his parents admonished him in the normal life of church going.

In due time, though he attached no particular meaning to it, William was confirmed in the Church of England. The historical books of the Bible attracted him in his reading, since he felt they were akin to the tales of travel of which he was so fond. He said in later years that this reading of the Bible brought "many stirrings of the mind. My mind was furnished with themes which afterwards were influential on my heart when I had a little leisure." He owed a debt of gratitude, he often said later, for the musical training he received as a choir-boy. He spoke of this in the years to come as "a lifelong enrichment."

Life was hard in those days, and when William was twelve the time came for him to earn at least a part of his living. Consequently, he left school and began work. Eager to follow in the footsteps of his hero uncle, he took up gardening. Greatly as he loved this work he was unable to continue it, for it caused a rash to break out on his face and hands which he called "a very painful trouble that defied a cure." Sleep became impossible because of the distress. He suffered this pain for two years — so keen was his interest in continuing his work with nature. Finally his health broke under the strain and he was compelled to admit defeat. One thing he did learn, however, as he said in later life, was that if one wants a straight furrow when plowing "he must set his eyes upon a definite mark."

This setting of his eyes upon a definite mark became the outstanding characteristic of William Carey's later life. Whatever he undertook there was always a goal to be achieved, an end to be accomplished. However great the intervening means, or troublesome the path, Carey knew that he must plow forward in a straight course to that end. This same determination made William Carey the sire of the modern missionary movement. When God planted his feet on India's soil, William, under divine leadership and holy inspiration, set goals seemingly impossible to attain. But by plowing with his hand to the Gospel plow, and steering a straight furrow to the end, William achieved those ends.

After a family council it was decided that William should learn shoemaking, fast becoming one of the principle industries of the country. With painstaking care Father Edmund sought for a man into whose home he could entrust the boy as an apprentice for seven years. Finally he selected Clark Nichols, of Piddington, a nearby village.

Nichols was not only a cobbler or mender of shoes, but was also a "cord-wainer," or maker of shoes. He made shoes from the soles on through to the completed task, so William Carey learned shoe-making as well as mending. While William made shoes he must have also learned the glory of a created task.

Nichols' reputation as a strict churchman and disciplinarian had recommended him to William's father. Upon association with the master, however, young William soon discovered Nichols' true character. Master Nichols was marked by a rough tongue and a bad temper. He was inclined to carouse on Saturday nights, and on Sunday morning he would send William to deliver shoes.

"A strict churchman and what I thought a very moral man," said William, in characterizing his master. "It is true he sometimes drank too freely and generally employed me in carrying out goods on the Lord's day morning, but he was an inveterate enemy of lies, a vice to which I was often addicted."

This discrepancy between profession and performance

soon disgusted William. Religion and its adherents, as he had come to know many of them, became obnoxious, and young Carey began to turn to loose companions and worldly pleasures. Nichols, however, had one redeeming possession which attracted William's attention, and that was a number of religious books. One of these, a New Testament commentary, had some strange characters in it that aroused William's curiosity.

When William asked Master Nichols what these characters were, the cobbler shook his head, for he did not know. Searching among his acquaintances for one who could tell him the meaning of those characters, William remembered there was a weaver in his home village, a man of education who had been reduced to poverty. This man might open the door to the true meaning of these strange characters. So William carried copies of the odd-looking characters found in this commentary to the educated, though irresolute, poverty-stricken weaver and asked what they meant.

The weaver told him that they were Greek letters. This in time led to Carey's seeking a Greek glossary and grammar, and shortly to his beginning a career which eventually led him to become one of the notable scholars of his day. William had shown an interest in language when he was still a boy in his father's school. Here he had mastered enough of Latin to translate an inscription on a famous tomb in the village church. Now this new interest had a further beneficial effect upon the young cobbler. It helped wean him from his companions, and from the life which was gradually leading him astray.

Also working in the Nichols' shop was a man from a neighboring village, by the name of John Warr. God doubtless planted John Warr near William Carey at this time so that the young man's spiritual life might be awakened. Carey shared the work bench during the day and an attic at night with his fellow apprentice, John. Warr was three years older than William and had known his trade from infancy, for his father and grandfather before him had been shoemakers. John's grandfather was more than a shoemaker, however. He was a Non-Conformist who had been instrumental in starting an independent church in Paulerspury.

Young Warr, though not yet a professing Christian, had heard much talk in his home and among his father's friends on the subject of the spiritual life and Non-Conformity. He was thoughtful and interested in religious matters.

Young Carey (and almost everyone else) disdained those people who at the time were called Dissenters or Non-Conformists. The children of the dissenters were banned from the Pury schools. Thus, though he and John were good friends, arguments flew between the two, Nichols, the master, sometimes joining in. The work would almost come to a stop as these discussions grew heated.

"I had, moreover, pride sufficient for a thousand times my knowledge," says William. "So I always scorned to have the worst in discussion, and the last word was assuredly mine. I always made up with positive assertions what was lacking in my reasoning, and generally came off with triumph. But I was often afterwards convinced that though I had the last word, my fellow apprentice had the better of the argument, and I felt a growing uneasiness and twinge of conscience gradually increasing. I had no idea that a complete change of heart was the only thing that would do me any good."

God, however, was preparing the fallow ground of William's soul, for there was to come a time of complete religious awakening, a reversal of his previous position, when Carey was to know that his soul had been remade by Christ coming into his life. The ground was now being prepared for that momentous occasion. John Warr was not arguing merely for the sake of delineations, contradiction and argument for argument's sake. He was really seeking God with all his heart and searching "for the Pearl of great price." Finally John found it, and once he was the possessor of this religious transformation and knowledge, he was eager to share his treasure not only with William but with Master Nichols.

"He became importunate with me, lending me books (for there were many such in his home), which gradually wrought a change in my thinking and my inward uneasiness increased," Carey related in later years.

God was gradually pointing out the path that William's life was to follow. There was a work for William Carey to do which would be impossible for him unless first he was spiritually born again. Once Carey realized that he *himself* had become a new creature in Christ Jesus, he would not rest content until he carried this knowledge to the teeming millions of India.

Warr's godly life continued to impress William, who sensed the sincerity, purity and the Christ-like love of his companion. Finally, after much insistence on John's part, William consented to attend a prayer meeting held by the Dissenters, and once there, he came under the spell of their spiritual fervor. He did not yield easily, however. To offset the influence of the Dissenters, William attended his own church more frequently. He did, however, "determine to leave off lying, swearing, and other sins to which I was addicted, and sometimes when alone I tried to pray."

A more drastic experience was needed to arouse him thoroughly and reveal to him the sinfulness of his unregenerate nature. In relating the incident that brought about his conversion, William said:

"A circumstance which I always reflect on with a mixture of horror and gratitude occurred about this time, which though greatly to my dishonor, I must relate. It being customary in that part of the country for apprentices to collect Christmas boxes (donations) from the tradesmen with whom their masters have dealings, I was permitted to collect these little sums. When I applied to an ironmonger, he gave me the choice of a shilling or a sixpence. I, of course, chose the shilling, and putting it in my pocket, went away. When I had a few shillings, my next care was to purchase some little articles for myself. But then to my sorrow I found that my shilling was a brass one. I paid for the things which I bought by using a shilling of my master's.

"I now found that I had exceeded my stock by a few pence. I expected severe reproaches from my master, and therefore came to the resolution to declare strenuously that the bad money was his. I well remember the struggles of mind which I had on this occasion, and that I made this deliberate sin a matter of prayer to God, as I passed over the fields toward home. I there promised that if God would but get me clearly over this, or, in other words, help me through with the theft, I would certainly for the future leave off all evil practices; but this theft and consequent lying appeared to me so necessary that I could not dispense with them.

"A gracious God did not get me safely through. My master sent the other apprentices to investigate the matter. The ironmonger acknowledged giving me the shilling, and I was therefore exposed to shame, reproach and inward remorse which preyed upon my mind for a considerable time.

"I trust that under these circumstances, I was led to see much more of myself than I had ever done before, and to seek for mercy with greater earnestness. I attended only prayer meetings, however, till February 10, 1779. This being appointed a day of fasting and prayer, I attended worship on that day. Mr. Chater, Congregationalist, of Olney, preached, but from what text I have forgotten. He insisted much on following Christ entirely, and enforced his exhortation with that passage, 'Let us therefore go out unto Him without the camp, bearing His reproach' (Heb. 13:13).

"I think I had a desire to follow Christ; but one idea occurred to my mind on hearing these words which broke me off from the Church of England. The idea was certainly very crude but useful in bringing me from attending a lifeless, carnal ministry to one more evangelical. I concluded that the Church of England, as established by law, was the camp in which all were protected from the scandal of the Cross, and that I ought to bear the reproach of Christ among the Dissenters, and accordingly, I have always attended divine worship among them."

The work had been done. William Carey had found the God who was to guide the forces of his life henceforth. Thus was brought about that important event which, as Samuel Vincent says, gave to the world, "a philanthropist, scholar, missionary and saint." Once William had made this decision he became a new man, one whose life was from that time forth wrapped up with the destiny of the Gospel, first in his own country and then in India.

William Carey had come to Christ a humble, insignificant, untutored youth. Christ gently placed the power of His glory upon the lad, and William is now looked upon as one of the most capable missionaries the church has ever known.

In Carey's conversion there came into the world one of the greatest influences for carrying the Gospel to the ends of the earth that had struck the stream of civilization since the beginning of the Christian era. William Carey in coming to Christ, became a missionary. His life became a fountain from which streams flowed forth into the unevangelized deserts of the world until at this writing, more than a century and a half later, much of the world has at least heard the story of redemption as a result of his labors.

Carey was still a shoemaker's apprentice, however. When he was eighteen, in September of 1779, his master died. Carey transferred his apprenticeship to Thomas Old in the village of Hackelton. Here on Sunday, June 10, 1781, at the age of twenty, he married Dorothy Plackett, the sister of his master's wife. Dorothy was five years older than he and not so well educated, for neither she nor her bridesmaid sister could sign their names. The family was evidently well thought of in the village, however, for her father was chief leader of "the meeting," and one of her sisters married one of its deacons.

When Master Old passed away, William assumed the business, taking upon himself the care of the widow and her four children. This was quite a responsibility for a man of twenty. To add to his income so he could carry the double load, William opened an evening school.

Meanwhile he was wrestling with many theological and spiritual problems which his new field of thought threw upon him. Thomas Scott, the noted biblical commentator, often stopped in at Carey's shop on his trip from Olney where he preached. Scott said of William:

"I observed the lad, who had entered with Mr. Old, riveted in attention with every mark and symptom of intelligence and feeling, saying little but modestly asking now and then an appropriate question. I took occasion, before I went forward, to inquire after him and found that, young as he was, he was a member of the church at Hackelton and looked upon as a very consistent and promising character. I called two or three times each year, and each time was more and more struck with the youth's conduct."

William says that Thomas Scott was a spiritual help to him. Scott was well fitted to inspire young Carey, for he had taught Latin, Hebrew and Greek. Likewise he was an ardent preacher and an earnest and influential student of the Bible. Years later William wrote of this association:

"If there be anything of the work of God in my soul I owe much of it to Mr. Scott's preaching when I first set out in the ways of the Lord."

Another spiritual aid in Carey's search for truth was a little volume entitled, "Help to Zion's Travelers — being an attempt to remove several stumbling blocks out of the way relating to Doctrinal, Experimental and Practical Religion." This was written by Robert Hall, father of the famous preacher, and a minister at Arnsby. The book attempted "to relieve discouraged Christians in the day of gloominess and perplexity so they might devote themselves to Christ through life, as well as be found in Him in death." William made a careful study of the treatise and wrote concerning it, "I do not remember ever to have read any book with such raptures."

Carey sought other Christians in Hackelton who shared his convictions. With them he discussed the religious problems and perplexities which he faced. With the aid of John Warr and some of these Hackelton Christian friends he started a Congregational church. He also traveled to nearby towns to hear the famous preachers who came to Northampton, Ravenshire and Roade. At the latter place he was greatly impressed by a sermon preached by a Baptist minister. Doubtless this sermon had much to do in influencing William to cast his lot with the Baptists, for he suddenly decided it was his religious duty to be baptized.

"I do not recollect having read anything on the subject, but I applied to Mr. Ryland, Sr., to baptize me. He lent me a pamphlet and turned me over to his son."

This son became a lifelong friend of William's, and was one of the staunchest supporters of Carey's work. When the famous Baptist Missionary Society held its first public meeting in London, Ryland told of William's baptism, saying:

"On October 5, 1783, I baptized in the River Nen, a little beyond Dr. Doddridge's meeting house at Northampton, a poor journeyman shoemaker, little thinking that before nine years had elapsed he would prove the first instrument of forming a society for sending missionaries from England to preach the Gospel to the heathen, and that . . . later he would become the professor of languages in an Oriental College, and the translator of the Scriptures in eleven different tongues. Such, however, as events have proved, was the purpose of the Most High who has selected for this work, not the son of one of our most learned ministers, nor one of the most opulent of our descending gentlemen, but the son of a parish clerk."

William Carey might have been a shoemaker, but from this moment on he was the anointed of the Lord, set aside for a definite task. God elevated and multiplied his capacities and abilities, making him in the end one of the greatest sons of the Church. Others might follow in his wake but he was a trail-blazer, like Livingstone in Africa, or Robert Morrison in China, or Henry Martyn in Persia.

Carey stands forth alone, however, as the first great modern missionary upon whom the beneficent outpourings of God were showered. Henceforth not Carey, but the Cross of Christ was elevated. He labored not in his own powers but in the strength and endowment of the Holy Spirit. He furnished the instrument, God the motivation, the empowerment. Carey handed God latent abilities unmarked for greatness, God multiplied them until they became the seedbed from which sprang missionary achievements seemingly impossible.

Chapter 2

DREAMING ON A COBBLER'S BENCH

CAREY, now in his early twenties, had planted his feet upon the Gospel path and was launched in his career. Rough edges in his character needed to be smoothed, dreams to be sparked into life, yet Carey had heard the voice of God commanding him to achieve, and he could not be content with less than his best for the Almighty.

Over the door of his shop was a sign which has been preserved in the college in Regent's Park. This is now partly illegible, but it reads, "Secondhand shoes bought and —." Over Carey's workbench in this humble shop was a crude map which William's hand had made of broad sheets of paper pasted together. On this map he had drawn with a pen the outline of the then known nations of the world and had written in the facts that he had gleaned about them from his extensive reading.

Thomas Scott, one of his best friends, called this humble workshop "Carey's College." As he sat at his workbench by the window where he could see his loved garden, Carey continued his studies of Latin and Greek, dipped into Hebrew, and as time went by added other languages. He borrowed books from anyone who would lend then and starved himself to buy books when opportunity offered. Among his borrowed books was an edition of *Captain Cook's Voyages*, which included fascinating illustrations. Here was a wealth of material which William enjoyed — adventure, exploration, strange stories of far-off people, weird customs, a botany of a new type. Carey eagerly pored over this material.

As he thought more deeply upon what he read, he began to see the conditions of these people. He recognized their pitiable ignorance of Christ and pondered on what His love would do for them. His heart was stirred. Within him arose a vague, wandering thought, which came and went as the days went by. Sometimes it paused to converse with Carey.

Carey was an extremely busy young man with all his home duties. He had his own family to care for. A little girl had been born into the home. She had been named Ann after Carey's loved grandmother. He contributed also to the support of the sister-in-law and her four children. In the evening he taught school. Since he was unable to submerge the spiritual ideals so dear to him in the purely material pursuit of shoemaking and teaching, he also began to preach.

He began speaking at first in the "little meeting" of the village. Evidently his efforts were well received for he said his hearers "sometimes applauded." He modestly explained this by saying they were "ignorant," and concluded this approval was "much to his great injury."

His interest in religious work led him into a conference at Olney, some ten miles distant. He walked to the conference, and being without money he was compelled to go without food the entire day. Here he met Andrew Fuller, the occasion for a momentous advance in both Carey and Fuller's lives. Fuller became one of Carey's staunch friends upon whom he could depend throughout life. Carey also met a Mr. Charver and others who asked him to preach at Earls Barton, a neighboring town. Later he accepted the invitation although it meant a walk of sixteen miles for him. (He was paid enough to cover the cost of the

clothes he wore out in this godly service). Carey recognized, however, that he was not preaching for financial
gain, but for the soul enrichment of both himself and his
hearers. Consequently his work as a minister began to take
on enlarging proportions. Always submerging the financial
to the spiritual, William Carey spoke to the hearts of those
who made up his congregations.

When those in his home town heard that Carey had been
preaching in the nearby village, he was asked to take the
local pulpit. His sister tells of this first sermon, for to
have the son of a staunch Anglican preaching for the
Dissenters was an event to stir the village.

"At this time he was increasingly thoughtful and very
jealous for the Lord of Hosts. When he came home, we
used to wonder at the change. We knew that before he
was rather inclined to persecute the faith he now wished to
propagate. He felt the importance of things to which we were
strangers. His natural disposition was to pursue earnestly
whatever he undertook, so that we did not wonder at it.
We marveled, however, at the change in him. After a
time, he asked permission to have family prayers when he
came home to see us, a favor which we very readily granted.

"A few of our friends of religion wished our brother to
exercise his rights by speaking to a few friends in a house
licensed at Pury which he did with great acceptance. The
next morning a neighbor of ours, a very pious woman, came
in to congratulate my mother on the occasion, and to speak
of the Lord's goodness in calling *her* son to a noble
calling.

" 'What, do you think he will be a preacher?'

" 'Yes, and a great one, I think, if spared.'

"From that time till he was settled at Moulton, he
regularly preached once a month at Pury with great acceptance. Our father much wished to hear his son, if he
could do it unseen by him or any one. An opportunity of-

fered and he embraced it. We were convinced he approved
of what he heard and was highly gratified by it."

Despite these growing activities Carey's thirst for knowledge did not abate. A book was always at hand as he
labored at his trade. As he took the shoes to his customers
in the surrounding towns, he pondered upon what he had
been reading. The times in which he lived were full of
events — sufficient to arouse both thought and argument.
The American colonies had thrown off the yoke of England
and were struggling toward a government "of the people,
by the people and for the people." Faint rumblings of a
movement toward freedom in France were beginning to be
heard. Sovereignty of the people and equal rights for all
men were the popular themes of the day.

Changes were taking place in matters other than government. The evils of the slave trade were being made known.
The ships in which the slaves were being transported were
"all floating hells." Children were advertised for sale in the
London papers. Carey, a lover of mankind who had, in
addition, heard the voice of God challenge his soul with the
message of redemption for all the world, was vehement
and outspoken against these evils. In his prayers he always referred to this "inhuman and accursed traffic."

Science and invention were opening a new world. Econo-
mists were pointing to better standards of business. Interest
in India was aroused by the trial of Warren Hasting. The
voyages of Captain Cook had lifted the eyes of the Englishmen beyond the horizon of their little island home. The
lives of Wesley, Whitfield, Doddridge and Wilberforce —
revivalists and song writers — all of these and many other
forces challenged Carey. His mind was awakened by this
vision of a new spiritual world, with more humane and
Christlike living.

Little wonder, then, that his keen mind was stirred to the
depths. At the same time there arose in his soul an ever-

expanding desire to put his shoulder to the Gospel wheel that he might help bring Christ to these new and distant places of the world.

For Carey all was not easy. Both he and his daughter fell ill of fever, and little Ann did not recover. This illness was followed by ague, from which Carey suffered for more than a year. His business consequently fell off. Often the little family lacked food. Finally William was led to move to the neighboring village of Moulton where there was a better opportunity for teaching.

On May 11, 1785, when William was twenty-four, he and his wife took up their residence in this little town perched on the high road between Kettering and Northampton, some four miles from the latter. At this time Carey was relieved of the care of his sister-in-law and her children. This lightened burden proved fortunate, for soon the former Moulton schoolmaster returned. Since he was a native of the village and also a Church of England man he naturally was better received and stood higher in the town's esteem than Carey, who had but shortly before taken up the task of schoolmastering among the villagers. Consequently many of the former teacher's pupils left Carey and returned to their previous instructor.

Carey, however, was not to be daunted by such an ill wind as this. He continued his school, and kept pace with his expenses by his shoemaking. He devoted all the time possible to training himself, realizing his own shortcomings. He recognized that to fill the place God had set before him, he must master not only himself, but useful knowledge to its broadest extent. He not only had his homemade map on the wall of his shop, but he fashioned a leather globe in different colors, the better to understand the far-away places of the earth. Recognizing the fact that knowledge was wrapped up in languages, he added French, Italian and Dutch to his own course of study.

William knew not what the wheels of time would turn up for his hands to do, but he did sense that to fill the place, humble or great, which God would mark for him, he must first be a prepared worker. Consecrating himself not only to the requirements of knowledge and the improving of his own native gifts, but also to the broad will of God, William Carey furnished his Heavenly Father with a workman that could stand in any field of the world, well prepared for the task at hand.

William embarked upon a new training course in Moulton as pastor of the local Baptist Church. At the time of his arrival, the church had been without a pastor for some time. The building was closed and dilapidated. When the members of the congregation asked him to preach, and he gave them his spare Sundays, the effects were soon seen. The membership awakened to its new task and took heart. Finally interest was renewed, and conversions became the order of Carey's services. After a short time the congregation formally invited him to become their stated pastor.

Here began a training which was to prove vital to the work of William Carey, necessitating a more formal recognition than he had been receiving as a lay minister. Consequently he applied for membership in the Olney Church, with the understanding that he would submit his fitness for the ministry to its judgment. He was accepted on these conditions, and on Sunday, July 17, 1785, he preached his trial sermon.

The congregation was large — some seven hundred — which was far more than he had ever addressed in one gathering before. His listeners were critical, since they came for the express purpose of measuring his ability as a minister. Before such an audience and feeling the importance of this trial message, Carey was probably nervous and embarrassed. It is certain, at least, that he did not speak to the best of his ability. The membership noticing this embarrassment, felt they could not recommend him. Their verdict read:

"Resolved that he should be allowed to go on preaching at those places where he had been for some time employed, and that he should be engaged again on suitable occasions some time before us in order that further trial may be made of his ministerial skill."

Carey, though sensing that this was a failure, did not recognize it as a termination of his preaching task. For the next year he spoke as occasion demanded, continued to pastor the local congregation at Moulton, and later with a message burning in his soul, again preached before the Olney membership. Carey, though full of his subject, failed in his own estimation and delivered as he said "a message as weak and crude as anything ever called a sermon." Evidently the massiveness of Carey's own thought and the depth of the message overshadowed what he considered the true worth of the sermon. This time the congregation accepted him and he was commissioned "to preach the Gospel wherever God in His providence might call him."

He was ordained at Moulton on August 1, 1786, in his twenty-fifth year. Three friends and fellow-ministers, Ryland, Sutcliff and Fuller, men who were to link their arms through faith with Carey's missionary adventures in the following years, officiated. A score or more of other ministers were present. Few if any of them realized that the young man before them was destined to become one of the most valuable workers in the Lord's vineyard. Ryland perhaps, glimpsed Carey's gifts, for he said once after having heard him preach, "I would I had a like deep sense of truth."

Even as the hands of the ministers were laid upon him, setting him apart for Christian service, more supremely did the anointing of God consecrate William Carey to the task of becoming the most famous missionary of his generation.

Carey returned to Moulton as pastor of the small congregation at a salary of approximately $75.00 per year. It was necessary for him to teach his school, small though it was, and to labor on as a shoemaker to augment his income. Deeming it wise to change his method of conducting his trade, Carey hired himself out to aid a shoemaker of Kettering named Thomas Gotch. Every two weeks the young preacher tramped to Gotch's place of business with the shoes which he had finished, returning home with the leather for the coming fortnight's work.

William enjoyed these walks, for they gave him time to ponder on the spiritual subjects which were ever dominating his thinking. Likewise they became hours of communion with God. As he walked he mused. He saw the great map of the world. His spiritual eyes picked out the far-away neglected nations that the world had slighted. As he thought and dreamed, he prayed that God would make it possible for him to do something about the fate of those nations yet in heathen darkness.

This new method of work not only relieved Carey of much anxiety and responsibility — it also brought about another blessing. Pastor Fuller, who had become interested in William's linguistic efforts, spoke to Gotch, who was a deacon in Fuller's church, about Carey's earnest and persevering pursuit of knowledge.

One day when Carey came to Gotch with a load of finished shoes, the master asked, "How much do you earn a week, Mr. Carey, by your shoemaking?" To which William replied, "About nine or ten shillings, sir."

Gotch's eyes twinkled as he said, "Well now, I've something to tell you. You needn't spoil any more of my leather, but get on as fast as you can with your Latin, Hebrew and Greek and I'll allow you from my private purse ten shillings a week."

William Carey's dream at length was coming true. He

had often longed to be free of shoemaking that he might
delve the deeper into the untapped reservoirs of knowledge.
His alert mental capacities, like long fingers, wanted to
reach out to those portions of truth which to him as yet
were a closed domain. Carey gladly accepted the ten shillings. Gotch was a banker of Kettering and a contractor to
the Army and Navy for footwear as well. With large
resources at hand he was willing to make this financial in-
vestment in the spiritual growth of the young minister.
He discerned unusual qualities in Carey, and the grant
which to William at the time seemed large, to Gotch was but
a tithe invested in kingdom enterprises.

Carey's service as pastor from this time on bore rapid
fruit. He looked upon his work as "the highest honor upon
earth."

The congregation grew and the meeting house had to be
enlarged. The people were stirred by the breath of the Holy
Spirit. Life moved to a quickened, kindlier tempo which
helped to brighten some of the dark days that came to the
little congregation and the village as well. Soon an epidemic of smallpox, followed by a malignant fever, perhaps
due to insufficient food and lack of proper sanitation carried
many away. Often in Carey's cottage, for instance, there
was no meat to eat for weeks at a time.

Busy as the pastor was with his studies and the work and
cares of his ministry, the wandering thought of the heathen
in other lands never left him. He came back more and more
frequently and persistently to that map with the unreached
nations of the world penciled upon it. As he studied, he
stored away in his memory facts about those countries, their
peoples and their strange customs.

Once when his fellow ministers, Hall, Ryland, Sutcliff
and Fuller, more learned and experienced than Carey,
were gathered in a ministers' meeting in Gotch's house, a
question arose about a small East Indian island. None

of those learned ministers knew anything about the place. Finally Carey arose modestly from a rear seat and gave not only the location of the island, but its size and character, and the religious beliefs of its people.

Almost unconsciously Carey had gone about making a survey of the task awaiting the church in heathen lands. When teaching geography lessons he would often exclaim with tears in his eyes, "And these are pagan, pagan!" With this knowledge of world conditions an integral part of his character, Carey was awakened to the growing demand of God upon the Church that these regions have the Gospel proclaimed to them.

William read the lives of John Eliot and David Brainerd, devoted missionaries to the North American Indians. He gloried in the work which these famed men had accomplished for God among the heathen.

"He was always remarkably impressed with heathen lands and the slave trade," his sister said, in noting the enlarging vision which God was placing on William's mind. "I never remember him engaging in prayer without praying for these poor heathen. The first time I ever recollect any feeling for the heathen world was from a discourse I heard my brother preach at Moulton from these words, 'For Zion's sake I will not hold my peace, and for Jerusalem's sake will I give him no rest.' "

As pastor at Moulton, Carey was admitted to the Ministers' Fraternal of the Northampton Association. Here in 1786 at a meeting he was asked to offer a subject for discussion. He proposed that they consider the problem which was nearest his own heart, "Whether the command given to the apostles to teach all nations was not binding on all succeeding ministers to the end of the world, seeing that the accompanying promise was of equal extent."

William's suggestion met with a harsh rebuke. Mr. Ryland, Sr., chairman, exclaimed:

"Young man, sit down! You are an enthusiast. When God pleases to converse with heathen He'll do it without consulting you or me. Besides, there must be another Pentecostal gift of tongues."

Carey felt that his knowledge of languages was his gift of tongues. He felt that God had given him this worldwide vision, though at the moment, as he later expressed it, he knew he had received "an abashing rebuke." He did not dismiss the subject from his thoughts. The Almighty had written it indelibly upon the walls of his mind. It dominated the screen of his vision. He discussed this worldwide vision with his fellow ministers — Fuller, Sutcliff and other neighboring preachers.

"They mostly regarded it," Fuller said, "as a wild impractical scheme, and gave him no encouragement."

In 1788, while on a trip to Birmingham on church business, Carey met Thomas Potts, who as a young man had been in America and had made friends among the Indians and Negroes. Potts had seen the evils of the slave trade, and as he and William Carey began to discuss Indians and slaves, they finally turned their attention to the problem of world missions.

At length Potts persuaded Carey to write a pamphlet on this subject to arouse Christians to the need of assuming their missionary obligations. William, encouraged by one who had seen missions in action in other lands, admitted that he would like to do it, but suggested that he was unequal to the task.

"Besides," he added, "if I could do it satisfactorily I could not afford to print it."

Potts arose to the occasion and exclaimed, "If you can't do it as you wish, do it as you can, and I'll give you ten pounds toward its printing."

Thus was launched a tangible missionary adventure. Indicative of his interest he said that though he felt diffident about writing a pamphlet upon the subject, he would not hesitate to go to the heathen whenever God might open the door, provided friends would support him for a year after his arrival. He expressed a preference for Tahiti or the South Seas, the results, perhaps, of Carey's having read Captain Cook's tales of his famous voyages.

God's hour for the modern missionary movement had not arrived, however, and the time for Carey's departure upon the great work of his life was not yet. He returned to Moulton where he began the task of arousing his own church to its missionary opportunity, as well as its spiritual obligation to the heathen. He was thankful that the allowance which Gotch gave him afforded him freedom from shoemaking so that he might invest his time in reading and reflecting. Out of this period sprang the plan for Carey's new missionary undertaking.

In the midst of all the malcontent in his own soul at the status of the Church with reference to the heathen world, Carey received a call from the church at Leicester. This church, called Harvey Lane, requested Carey to become its pastor. From a worldly point of view this new opening was assuredly an improvement upon his present position. Leicester was a far more important town than Moulton. The church had a larger membership, the meeting house was more impressive and the salary quite an improvement upon Carey's present meager $75.00 annual stipend. But worldly consideration weighed little in Carey's estimation. Harvey Lane did, however, present quite different problems from Moulton.

For several weeks Carey weighed the matter. He sought advice from friends. Andrew Fuller said, "In his statement of the case there was much of the devout and uprightness of God."

Carey made one of the most important decisions of his life only after a prayerful consideration of his spiritual motives. Fighting this problem through, required serious thought. He knew that the Leicester Church had fallen into evil ways. Dissension and recrimination were rife among the members. Drinking was prevalent, with addicts even among the church officials. The previous pastor had taken no steps to improve the matters. He had resigned and his membership in the church had been cancelled. Members of the Church of England in that town lamented the disgrace that Harvey Lane was bringing upon so-called religion. After long and prayerful consideration, in the spring of 1789, Carey decided to accept the challenge.

For some time all went well; the congregation grew. "Our membership was so increased by the first quarter end," said a member, "that there was not room to sit conveniently." The increasing crowds coming to hear Carey's impassioned preaching required that a gallery be built at the cost of $500; a large sum to these poor people at the moment. Still they rallied to the task and built with enthusiasm. The malcontent members of the congregation had not given up, however. Soon they began criticizing their minister's spiritual endeavors. Some fell into their former bad habits and attendance dropped. It almost broke Carey's heart. He told Fuller that he was "distressed beyond measure at the trial of the situation."

God was challenging the mettle of Carey's soul in another matter. This trial was a new course in the curriculum of studies which Carey must master before God would place him on the mission field. Though he might have cast longing eyes back to Moulton with its peace and good fellowship, having once placed his hands to the Harvey Lane plow, Carey would not turn back. For two years he labored under these unhappy circumstances, and then in September of 1790 he proposed that the church be dissolved, and that it be re-established on a solemn covenant "to bind them to a strict and faithful New Testament discipline, let it afflict whom it might." At length this re-organization was accomplished. From that time on Harvey Lane was never again a "problem child" among the churches of the community.

During this time Carey continued his studies and devoted much effort to writing the pamphlet on the subject of carrying the Gospel to the heathen. He planned a regular schedule for study. On Monday he devoted time to the classics. On Tuesday science engaged his attention along with history and composition or writing. The rest of the week was given over to mastering Hebrew, Greek and delving into the treasures of the Bible. Leicester boasted several men interested in the broader fields of learning. Contact with them whetted Carey's desire.

The town also had an association of scientists. This association regularly called in lecturers, explorers and speakers who were primarily interested in humanitarian projects. These men were of different and varied religious beliefs. In these meetings Carey came in contact with some of the famous people of his generation. Here, for instance, he heard Howard, the father of prison reform, address the audience on the subject nearest his heart. Likewise, the young pastor attended the lectures delivered by a famous botanist, Brewin. Similarly, Carey met the famous musical composer, Gardner, who was interested in astronomy as well. All these contacts were stimulating and broadening. Young Carey became a welcomed member of this group of scientists and thinkers.

Carey has been described as having the appearance and manners of a peasant. He was short in stature and usually dressed poorly. His hands were those of a shoe cobbler and often were stained by the dyes of his trade. He wore a wig because an illness had left him bald. The wig was ill-fitting and stiff. The inner brightness of William Carey's spirit shown through his rustic exterior, however. Cultured men accepted him as their equal.

In 1791 Carey read his pamphlet to a select group of friends. The book was entitled, "An Enquiry into the Obligations of Christians to Use Means for the Conversion of Heathen in which the Religious State of the different Nations of the World, the Success of Former Undertakings, and the Practical Ability of further undertakings are Considered." The manuscript consisted of eighty-seven pages, the result of eight years of thought, study and composition. It was marked with a profound knowledge of geographical facts and racial conditions. It showed an acquaintance with the religious problems of the heathen world. Every known part of the world was considered, and accurate information (as accurate as could then be gleaned) was afforded. Islands of but a few square miles in area were considered as carefully as larger areas.

"Surely," Carey concluded, "it is worth laying ourselves out with all our might in promoting Christ's kingdom."

The pamphlet was published and sold for approximately thirty-five cents. It was a literary masterpiece, and has been called the "charter of modern missions," and "the distinct point of departure in the history of Christianity." This was the spark which fired into life the burning embers of missionary zeal that God had laid in Carey's soul. The booklet was the screen upon which William Carey projected the vast panorama of heathen conditions God had afforded him. In it Carey laid bare his own soul. He showed how God had burned indelibly upon his thinking that the command to go, as well as the promised companionship of Christ, was no more obligatory upon the apostolic church than upon the church of his century.

As a result of the pamphlet's publication and Carey's own continued agitation on the subject, the fiery pastor was asked to preach one of the association's sermons at the next meeting at Nottingham, May 30, 1792. This date must be marked in red on the calendars of the world. William spoke from the text, *Enlarge the place of thy tent, and let them stretch forth the curtains of thine habitations: spare not, lengthen thy cords, and strengthen thy stakes, For thou shalt break forth on the right hand and on the left, and thy seed shall inhabit the Gentiles, and make the desolate cities to be inhabited* (Isaiah 54:2, 3).

Carey's appeal was fervent, and the impression he made upon the audience was profound. He threw his whole being into it. The fire of his thought was summed up in these ringing words, *"Expect great things from God. Attempt great things for God."* The challenge was a stirring one. Carey impressed upon the minds of his Baptist brethren the fact that they could not deny God's command to preach the Gospel to the entire world.

After the various business affairs of the association had been finished and it became necessary to take up the appeals of Carey, "the old feelings of doubt prevailed, and they were about to separate without any decisive results, till Carey was in an agony of distress," as one member later expressed himself.

Turning to Fuller he asked tragically, "Is there nothing again going to be done, sir?" The heartbreak in Carey's voice, the fire which pierced through the words, stabbed Fuller awake. He asked for a reopening and a reconsideration of the subject which at the moment had been shelved. As a result of Fuller's championship of the issue, a famous resolution was passed which read:

"Resolved that a plan be prepared against the next ministers' meeting at Kettering for forming a Baptist Society for the propagating of the Gospel among the heathen."

Carey had won. The vision which God had given him had sparked into life among his Baptist brethren who were then present. When the next meeting at Kettering convened on October 2, 1792, in Carey's thirty-first year, there were those present who still expressed doubt of the outcome. Some wished to procrastinate about taking the great step. They recognized that this was a large undertaking, for they themselves were few, poor and little known. Carey told what others as humble as themselves had done. He outlined especially the achievements of the Moravians, and he discoursed upon the accomplishments of those who had given themselves to missionary work among the Negroes and the North American Indians.

"Can't we Baptists," he urged, "at least attempt something in fealty to the same Lord?"

Andrew Fuller, Ryland, Sutcliff and a fellow minister by the name of Pearce accepted Carey's challenge, and finally this resolution was adopted:

"Humbly desirious of making an effort for the propagation of the Gospel among the heathen according to the recommendations of Carey's 'Enquiry,' we unanimously resolve to act in Society together for this purpose, and as in the divided state of Christendom each denomination by exerting itself separately seems likeliest to accomplish the great end, we name this the Particular Baptist Society for the Propagation of the Gospel among the Heathen."

Thus the first modern missionary society came into being — the Baptist Missionary Society was formed. James Montgomery called this "a spark dropped from heaven." Another phrased it, "Thus the grand deeds grew that once were only dreams — dreams of a cobbler at his workbench with a crude map of the world fashioned by himself on the wall before him, and his Bible at his side." The dreams of the cobbler were soon to become living realities etched in bold outline upon the map of India in Carey's own blood and the blood of those who followed him.

Chapter 3

LAUNCHING THE MODERN
MISSIONARY MOVEMENT

THE MISSIONARY SOCIETY was now definitely organized.
Before the Kettering meeting broke up Andrew Fuller was
appointed secretary, and a Mr. Hogg, of Thrapston, became the first treasurer. An offering was made by the
brethren present which amounted to approximately sixty-
five dollars — a small sum measured in light of the tremendous undertaking and the worldwide organization for
which Carey's program called. Shortly thereafter, Mr.
Pearce obtained $350.00 from friends in Birmingham. At
the same time the committee drew up a letter which they
"addressed to their fellow Christians at large."

This letter of intent to attack the problem of world evangelization faced the committee with an important question,
"What part of the heathen world shall receive our immediate attention?" Allied questions of great moment were,
"Where is the most promising opening to be obtained?" and,
"Where shall a suitable missionary or missionaries be
found?" Carey wrote the committee a short time later
saying:

"I have just received a letter from Mr. Thomas, the
Bengal missionary, who informs me that he intended being
at the Kettering meeting, but forgot the date. He tells me
that he is trying to establish a fund in London for a mission
to Bengal; he earnestly desires a companion, and inquires

about the result of our Kettering meeting. The reason for
my writing is a thought that his fund for Bengal may interfere with our larger plan; and whether it would not be
worthy of the Society to try and make that and ours unite
into one fund for the purpose of sending the Gospel to the
heathen indefinitely."

In this letter William Carey laid bare his own soul, for
he set aside all his own desires, and particularly the dream
or aspiration of being the Society's first missionary, and his
long-cherished wish to go to Tahiti.

The Society decided to consider the proposal, and Andrew
Fuller was appointed to look into John Thomas' credentials.
The insignificant phrase in Carey's letter stating that
Thomas had forgotten the time of the Kettering meeting,
gave an indication of the true character of the man. Thomas
was impetuous, bubbling with enthusiasm, and optimistic.
As a youth in Glouchestershire, he had run away to London
where he studied medicine. Shortly thereafter he went to
Calcutta as a surgeon for the East India Company. He had
ventured into various areas of the mysterious land of India.
Although full of the zest of life, he was always in debt
during his stay there.

In India he was converted and entered the Lord's service with the same wholeheartedness he had shown in his
previous adventurous life as a doctor. He gloried in
preaching "in and out of season" on the East India Company's boats, as well as in Calcutta.

In Calcutta the wretchedness of the native population tore
at Thomas' heartstrings. He devoted himself wholeheartedly
to them, treating the sick, giving to the poor as far as he
was able, mastering the language so he could aid them and
translating the Gospels of Matthew and Mark into Bengali.
Thomas soon gained the support of some English residents

in Bengal. Among them was Charles Grant and George
Udney. Finally, as Fuller discovered, the young doctor
decided to devote himself entirely to mission work in India.
He returned to England to secure money and to get his
wife and daughter.

"I could do anything for Christ," he wrote. "I would
suffer shipwreck and death to glorify Him but a little,
but if He should tear me from the Indians then I would be
a-bleeding, for my soul is set upon them."

This was the man that Andrew Fuller presented to the
Society for consideration as their representative. Fuller
suggested that it might be possible that Carey serve as
Thomas' colleague.

The Society met January 10, 1793, with Thomas present.
He graphically portrayed for them the poverty, ignorance
and superstition in Bengal and the work being done. He
mentioned the converts that had already been won, especially three Brahmin who had sent a letter to him, pleading,
"Have compassion on us and send us preachers, and such
as will forward translations." This call from India struck
to the core of Carey's heart. A desire was born which
could not be extinguished, namely, giving the Gospel to the
Indians in their native languages. In the end Carey devoted
his lifetime to it.

When the Society asked about living costs in Bengal,
Thomas enthusiastically assured them that living was cheap,
and that the missionary could support himself. When the
Society at length accepted Thomas as their representative,
Carey volunteered to go as his companion. The delighted
Thomas sprang enthusiastically to his feet and fell upon
Carey's neck with tears of joy.

Later, Fuller said of the momentous occasion, "We saw
that there was a gold mine in India, but it was as deep as

the center of the earth. I asked, 'Who will venture to explore it?' Carey replied, 'I will venture to go down, but remember that you' meaning Sutcliff, Ryland and myself, 'must hold the ropes.' We solemnly engaged ourselves to him to do so, and while we live shall we desert him?"

Thus was born that famous expression, "I will go down into the mine, but you must hold the ropes." These *rope-holders* nobly kept their pledge through long, trying years. The venture was laid out, and Bengal or India became the field to which the Society was henceforth to devote its attention. Although Carey's thoughts had been set on Tahiti, he admitted that by nature, training and his own mental gifts, he was better fitted for this broader field. His co-worker too, though impulsive, improvident and thoughtless in some ways, was bent with all of the intensity of his being upon bringing the light of the Gospel to the Hindus.

Though the movement was launched, it was not all to be clear sailing. Obstacles immediately developed. The first and most serious of these was the opposition of Carey's wife. She was expecting an addition to the family within the next few months making it impossible for her to go immediately. Furthermore, since she had never seen the sea, she was so fearful of it that she did not want to go at all. She could not face the thought of crossing the ocean to so distant a land, nor did she wish to leave her friends or family. Likewise she was unwilling that her husband should go.

Carey was quite firm in his stand, however. Knowing that this was the will of God, he sustained himself with the passage, "He that loveth wife or child more than me is not worthy of me."

He wrote a letter to his father on January 17, 1793, expressing his unshaken purpose:

"The importance of spending our time for God alone is the principal theme of the Gospel . . . To be devoted like a sacrifice to holy uses is the great business of a Christian. I therefore consider myself devoted to the sole service of God, and now I am appointed to go to Bengal in the East Indies, a missionary to the Hindus . . . My wife and family will stay behind at present . . . I hope, dear father, you may be enabled to surrender me to the Lord for the most arduous, honorable, and important work that ever any of the sons of men were called to pursue. I have many sacrifices to make. I must part with a beloved family, and a number of most affectionate friends . . . but I have set my hand to the plow."

The letter stunned Carey's father, who said of Carey's decision, "It was the folly of one mad." He could not believe that his son William would persist in what was to him an utterly inane desire.

Carey at length broke the news to his church. Here again he encountered intense opposition. Finally one member pointed out, "God is bidding us make the sacrifice. Let us rise to His call and show ourselves worthy." This challenge was tearfully accepted by his church, and their consent, along with their blessings, went out to Carey.

Meanwhile preparations for the venture moved steadily forward. Carey and Thomas visited nearby churches in deputation work, describing the greatness of the undertaking and soliciting funds to underwrite the attempt. On one of these trips Carey met a printer and newspaper editor, William Ward, and said to him:

"If the Lord bless us we will want a person of your business to print the Scripture. I hope you will come after us."

This proved to be a prophetic utterance, for within five years Ward had joined Carey in India.

On March 20, 1793, the missionaries were "set apart" like Barnabas and Paul, at the Harvey Lane Church, one of Carey's former and best-loved pastorates. The service consisted of prayer, preaching and a heartfelt parting charge based on Christ's words, "Peace be unto you. As my father hast sent me even so I send you," delivered by Andrew Fuller. This address made the day one of memorable blessing for Carey.

Carey's family, consisting now of three boys and his wife, (the two girls having passed away) were settled in Piddington, his wife's native village. Here they lived with her sister Kitty. At the last moment, Carey's wife was willing to allow the oldest boy, Felix, to go with his father.

Further difficulties must be braved, however. The charter of the East India Company was before Parliament for revision. Protests were being made over permits for "schoolmasters and missionaries" to labor under the Company. The uproar over the matter was at its height when Carey and Thomas sought their permit to sail to India and labor with and under the Company's blessing. They were advised by counsel that to ask for permit as missionaries would be to have the door closed in their faces. But they could not wait indefinitely.

Finally the captain of the *SS Earl of Oxford,* on whose ship Thomas had been ship's surgeon, agreed to take them without a permit. This was a hazardous move on the part of the missionaries, for if they were discovered it meant immediate return to England and the confiscation of their goods. Carey and Thomas were determined in their purpose, however, for they felt that they were launched in a work which had been ordained of the Lord, and they were willing to risk the necessary challenge. Consequently, on April 4, 1793, they boarded the vessel.

Carey, after many years of preparation, finally was approaching his great missionary adventure. He had read of the sea; he had mastered the geography of the nations of the earth; he had dreamed of such a venture under the tutelage of Captain Cook; but now he was undertaking a voyage that was to exceed in grandeur and importance any voyage which the famous Captain Cook had ever undertaken.

Hoisting anchor, the ship sailed to Portsmouth, where it was delayed for six weeks waiting for a convoy. At this period in England's history, pirates were the scourge of the seas. Another problem to be faced was Thomas' past debts. London creditors were dunning him to settle them. All this brought great humiliation upon Carey. Soon, however, he laid these perplexing problems — which seemed so momentous, but in reality were merely irksome — upon the broad shoulders of the Almighty, the best place to cast his burdens.

Carey received one item of good news at this time. A little son, whom his wife named Jabez was born in his cottage home. She named him Jabez "because she bore him with sorrow." Writing to Dorothy from the Isle of Wight, May 6, 1793, Carey said:

"I have just received yours, giving me an account of your safe delivery. This is pleasant news indeed to me; surely goodness and mercy follow me all my days. My stay here was very painful and unpleasant, but now I see the goodness of God in it. It was that I might hear the most pleasing accounts that I possibly could hear respecting earthly things . . . If I had all the world, I would freely give it all to have you and my children with me, but the sense of duty is so strong as to overpower all other considerations. I cannot turn back without guilt on my soul. I find a longing to enjoy more of God; but, now that I am among the people of the world, I think I see more beauties in godliness than ever, and I hope to enjoy God more in retirement than I have done for some time past."

Further complications arose which wrecked the two missionaries' departure schedule. The captain of the vessel received an anonymous letter from the East India House telling him that a passenger was sailing without permit, and that his captain's license would be revoked should the vessel carry such a person. Alarmed at this news the captain ordered Thomas and Carey to leave the ship. Carey, however, believed this was a ruse of one of Thomas' creditors to detain them. Thomas rushed off to London to investigate, but he was unsuccessful. The vessel sailed, taking Thomas' wife and daughter, but leaving Thomas, Carey and his son Felix, and all their baggage. It was a disconsolate trio that paced the dock when they realized that they had been outwitted by the captain. Carey wrote Fuller, saying:

"I have just time to inform you that all our plans are entirely frustrated for the present . . . All I can say in this affair is that however mysterious the leadings of Providence are, I have no doubt but that they are superintended by an infinitely wise God. I have no time to say more."

Carey knew that this delay was a divine providence, the intent of which at the moment he could not unravel. As events proved later, the delay made it possible for his family to sail with him.

The three returned to London, Carey's heart the heaviest of all. Still his determination to reach India did not wane. "I would undergo all the perils of an overland journey from Holland to Hindustan if necessary," he affirmed, "but the effort at present seems to be a failure." Andrew Fuller almost despaired of ever completing the plans to open India to the Gospel.

"We are all undone," Fuller wrote Ryland. "I am afraid now leave will not be obtained for Carey or another. The adventure seems to be lost."

God had a more gracious design than the failure of this noble attempt, however. Thomas flung himself with his usual impetuosity into the problem of surmounting these vexing difficulties. The season for vessels to depart for the Orient was drawing to a close. Thomas acted as if inspired. He hurried into a familiar coffee shop and asked the waiter if he knew of any Swedish or Danish vessels that were sailing for the East. The waiter gave him an address and Carey and he raced to it. Here they found that a Danish East India ship with vacant cabins was daily expected at Dover.

This was glorious news indeed, for a Danish vessel would doubtless be bound for the Danish settlement at Serampore, near Calcutta. When the missionaries asked the price of transport the answer was, "One hundred pounds ($500) for adults, fifty pounds ($250) for children and twenty-five pounds ($125) for attendants." When Carey and Thomas faced the problem of securing $500 each for themselves, and $250 for young Felix, the passage money seemed to be out of the question. They had only 150 pounds, or approximately $750, that had been refunded them by the captain of the vessel on which they were first to have sailed.

Once more hope seemed to vanish. Thomas and Carey went on trusting God to obliterate these difficulties, however. They looked to Him to accomplish the seemingly impossible. Thomas, humble man that he was, insisted that Carey and Felix take the $750 and sail. But Carey would not hear of this. Though the time was short the three rushed to Northampton to see if the money could not be raised. Carey even prayed that his wife could be persuaded to sail to India. He approached her with the suggestion. "With a baby scarcely a month old, three boys under nine, how could she be expected to get ready at a day's notice for a voyage to India," Dorothy demanded. She said the thought was preposterous.

With Dorothy's refusal ringing in his ears, Carey and his companions started on to Northampton. Thomas was not to be daunted, however. He said, "I'm going back, for I believe I can persuade her." So eloquently did he plead with Dorothy not to separate a family, and face lifelong regrets, that finally she consented to go, provided her sister Kitty would likewise undertake the voyage.

With this hurdle out of the way, the great difficulty now was money. Like a bursting tornado Thomas and Carey swept into Ryland's office in Northampton and laid the situation before him. They said they must have at least two hundred pounds.

"Impossible!" exclaimed Ryland. "I have only about twenty-five pounds, (about $125)."

Upon further thought, however, Ryland recalled that he had a certificate for $1000 which was not yet negotiable, but upon which the money could be advanced. He consented to do this. With the money in hand Carey and Thomas returned to Piddington where they hurriedly disposed of Carey's furniture. They packed immediately and left for London on the following day.

Thomas estimated that even with this money they had not enough now to finance the voyage, so he proposed if Kitty were willing, that he and she go as attendants to William and Dorothy. Kitty willingly consented to this scheme. Thus the group saved $350, for it must be remembered that attendants could sail for $125 instead of the usual $500 passage fee.

In London, friends of the mission venture contributed toward the purchase of the necessities for the long voyage. Thomas soon presented himself at the ship's office with his enlarged party, much to the amazement of the officials, and he told them of the amount of the money on hand, and of his own and Kitty's willingness to go as attendants. In amazement and admiration, the ship's officers accepted the money in full payment for passenger accommodations for the entire group!

When the Steamship *Kron Princess Maria* finally sailed from Dover on Thursday, June 13, 1793, William Carey and his wife Dorothy, their sons Felix, William, Peter and baby Jabez, along with Kitty and Thomas, were in the company. Thus the divine reason of the first vessel's sailing without them was finally understood by the missionaries. Once more God had made the wrath of men to praise Him. Carey wrote that evening in his diary:

"This has been a day of gladness to my soul. I was returned that I might take all my family with me and enjoy all the blessings which I had surrendered to God. This 'Ebenezer' I raise. I hope to be strengthened by its every remembrance."

Thus the first English-speaking missionary party sailed away from the white cliffs of Dover to blaze a missionary trail upon which many would later plant their feet. The light which Carey kindled spread from hill to hill like beacon flames until all Christendom in turn recognized the signal and responded to the missionary call.

A voyage to India in the 1790's was vastly different from a similar one today. The trip took five months. The vessel upon which the party sailed was small in comparison to

ocean liners of the present, but the captain who owned the
ship was, according to Carey, "a wide reader and one
of the most polite and accomplished gentlemen that ever
bore the name of a sea captain." He gave the Careys the
largest cabin — a pleasant room with windows and papered
walls. Part of this was partitioned off for Kitty.

The entire party was welcomed at the captain's table.
The fellow passengers were a mixture of various nationalities. Their racial peculiarities delighted Carey. Christian
services were held in Carey's cabin morning and evening,
and more especially on Sundays. In the tropics Carey fell
seriously ill, but the hand of God was shortly laid with a
healing touch upon this brave missionary. Carey at times
bewailed his own "spiritual inadequacy, the inconstancy of
his companion, and spent much time in prayer." He studied
Bengali with Thomas, and assisted the latter with his translation of Genesis into the language of Bengal.

During the last month while the ship was detained in
the Bay of Bengal by adverse currents Carey wrote the
Mission Society:

"I hope you will go on and increase, and that multitudes
may hear the glorious words of Truth. Africa is but a little
way from England; Madagascar but a little further; South
America and all the many and large islands in the Indian
and Chinese Seas will, I hope, not be forgotten. A large
field opens on every side, and millions tormented by ignorance, superstition and idolatry plead with every heart
that loves God. Oh, that many laborers may be thrust into
the vineyard, and the Gentiles come to the knowledge of
the Truth!"

India at the time, in the words of J. W. Kaye, was "a
closed preserve in the hand of the East India Company. To
go there without a license from the Company was to be-

come a poacher, and to incur the risk of being igno-
miniously sent home. A man without a covenant was in the
Company's estimation a dangerous person, doubly dangerous
was such a one with a Bible."

Carey and Thomas were well aware of this attitude on
the part of the East India Company. So now shortly after
the vessel entered the Hoogly River, and while laying at
Balasore, they decided to go ashore in a native boat and test
their reception. For the first time Carey heard the noise of
an Indian market and saw its busy life and glimpsed the
native costumes. For three hours Thomas preached to the
natives in their own language, much to their astonishment.
They were not accustomed to being addressed by a white
man. The natives listened attentively and later served the
missionaries a meal. Their interest and kindness filled
Carey with hope for a blessed future among them.

Unmolested, the party continued to Calcutta where they
landed November 11, 1793. They disposed of the goods
that had been brought as a trading venture and were ready
to launch their missionary endeavors. Carey had never been
among such swarms of people. He estimated that he was
surrounded by 200,000 in Calcutta and near-by districts.
He wrote of these first impressions:

"I feel something of what Paul felt when he beheld
Athens and 'his spirit was stirred within him.' I see one of
the finest countries in the world, full of industrious inhabitants; yet three-fifths of it is an uncultivated jungle,
abandoned to wild beasts and serpents. If the Gospel
flourishes here, the 'wilderness will in every respect become
a fruitful field.' "

He had not yet come into contact with the religious beliefs of the people. He had scarcely touched the fringe of
this garment. When Carey arrived in India the Hindus were
in a pitiably backward condition. Learning had almost

ceased, and ordinary educational facilities scarcely existed.
Spiritual religion was only to be met in the quietest places.
Idolatry and immoral rites dominated all the great centers
of population.

It was a dark picture. The interior jungles infested with
serpents and wild beasts were mild in comparison with
the moral jungles which these brave pioneers faced. But
Carey was young — then nearing thirty-three — so he and
Thomas sturdily took up their work. To live less expensive-
ly they moved up the river to Bendal, a Portuguese settlement. Here they met a Swede by name of Kiernander, who
was then in his eighties, an early and devoted missionary
whose influence among the natives had been most beneficial. He was, however, none too hopeful of success for
the new recruits.

Undaunted by the untoward predictions of the old
Swedish missionary, Thomas and Carey went about the
business of the Master. Daily they visited the villages,
Thomas preaching in the native tongue, Carey listening and
learning. They were attended by Ram Basu, one of Thomas'
earlier converts, who during the missionary's absence had
returned, under duress to his idols. Now he once more
took up the cloak of the Gospel and renewed his vows to
God. The three men were an amazement to the Hindus.
They flocked to hear and see; and went away talking among
themselves. Concerning these early experiences Carey wrote:

"Their attention is astonishing. Every place presents a
pleasing prospect of success. To see people so interested, in-
quisitive and kind, yet so ignorant, is enough to stir up any
one who has the love of Christ in his heart.

"Last Sunday, Mr. Thomas preached to nearly two hundred in a village. They listened with great seriousness, and
several followed to make further inquiries of the heavenly
way. The encouragements are very great. I never found

more satisfaction than in this undertaking. I hope in a little while to see a Church formed for God."

Carey was attracted by the religious sincerity of the people. He watched their morning purification baths in a river or pool. He noted their physical suffering, often in shivering temperatures for the sake of their souls' demands. "I have already seen several," he wrote friends, "who have swung by the flesh-hooks." The appalling number in need of spiritual enlightenment greatly stirred him. "Ten thousand ministers could find scope for their powers," he avowed, visualizing the teeming multitudes that waited for the light of Christ.

Bendal, being a Portuguese settlement was inhabited by a mixed population. Carey believed a place more purely Indian would better serve their purpose. Hence it was decided to go to Nadia, the "Hindu Oxford" of Bengal.

"Here," he wrote in his journal, "several of the most learned Pundits and Brahmin wished us to settle. As Nadia is the great place for eastern learning we seemed inclined to do so, especially since it is the bulwark of heathenism. If it receives the gospel all the rest of the country must be laid open to us."

Carey was well received by the scholarly Hindus who recognized his linguistic ability. He looked forward with joy to his own work. His boys were going to learn Sanskrit, Persian and Chinese. These pleasant dreams suddenly dissolved into flimsy vapor, for his wife and Felix were taken down with dysentery, his wife so seriously that Carey despaired of her life.

No land for cultivation was available at this settlement. Farming had been a part of Carey's overall plan for self-support. Money was running low. At this time Thomas was recalled to Calcutta because of pressing debts. Here he

resumed his medical practice so that he could earn enough
to liquidate his obligations. At this moment when the prospects were indeed gloomy, and the outlook overcast with
discouragement, Carey received what at the time seemed
a good offer, the superintendency of the Calcutta Botanical
Gardens. The captain of the vessel upon which the Careys
had come to India had convinced the officials that Carey was
the man to fill the place. Carey hurried to the city, only to
find that someone else had been appointed.

Carey was going through the crucible of God's testing.
The modern missionary movement was not to be launched
easily and lightly. Carey was to taste despair and de-
spondency. He was to meet all the vexations which the
hordes of missionaries that should follow him were to experience. He was to prove once and for all that "our
God is able." Dark days descended upon the family. Their
money was gone. Thomas had optimistically miscalculated
the expenses, and the funds supposed to last for a year
were barely sufficient for a few months. Mrs. Carey and
Felix were seriously ill. Carey himself had as yet found
no means of earning any money. A dilapidated garden
house in a marshy malarial district close to Calcutta was
offered to Carey rent-free by Datta, a money lender, and a
friend of Ram Basu. The Careys' condition was deplorable
indeed. They found the place to be scarcely habitable.

They were in a strange country where they could scarcely speak the language. They were penniless, without food;
Mrs. Carey was sick. There were the helpless children, and
the little baby. Carey walked miles in the Indian sun to see
the chaplain of Ft. William, a friend of one of his own
acquaintances in England, to ask him for help. Because of
Carey's connection with Thomas the man would give him
no help. "He did not even ask me to take refreshments,"

said Carey of the experience. The terrible testing through
which the Careys went at this time laid a troublesome
hand upon Dorothy's mind, the outcome of which was her
later mental disorder.

The convert Basu finally secured some land which they
could have for three years rent free. The land was located
in Sunderbunds. Money was secured from a lender and the
family boarded a boat for the three-day trip down the
Hoogly to the tiger-haunted and snake-infested swamps
near the mouth of the river.

On February 6, 1794, with but enough food for one meal,
the family landed at Dechatta. They had been promised
that they could occupy the Salt Department bungalow if
vacant, but unhappily it was not vacant at the time. Be-
wildered, not knowing where to turn, with scarcely any
food for a sick wife and family, William Carey seemed to
have reached the depth of disaster. There was one avenue
of succor and he turned to that. Carey lifted his voice in
trust and faith to the Almighty. Shortly thereafter aid came
from an unexpected source.

One day William was out for a walk when he was ac-
costed by Charles Short, an assistant in the Salt Department
of the India Company. Short was amazed when he saw
William Carey and heard the pitiable tale of the distressed
family. He took them to his own house and "insisted upon
supplying all their wants." God had not failed William
Carey, and this generous bachelor-Samaritan was in time
richly rewarded for his helping hand.

God thus taught Carey the lesson that when all human
efforts were unavailing, when all supplies were exhausted,
when there was no food in the larder nor money in the
treasury, that help was as near as the heavenly approach to
the throne of God. Carey never forgot this lesson during

all his years in India. Even though sometimes he could not humanly succeed he knew that with God all things are possible.

With his hand in God's and his mind fixed upon things above, William Carey dauntlessly faced his tomorrows in India.

Chapter 4

GIVING INDIA THE BIBLE

CAREY'S VISION of giving the Gospel to India held him firm through a series of perplexing difficulties. God had planted his feet on India's soil, and at any cost, however great the risk, he was God's missionary for the hour. He was in his element. He loved village life, and from his youngest childhood had been interested in the cultivation of the soil. Certainly the village where he now lived was vastly different from his native English hamlet, and the land, instead of the placid countryside of his own childhood and youth, was a matted jungle swarming with alligators, snakes and tigers. But Carey went joyfully to the task of making a home.

By selling timber he cleared from the land, wax from the wild beehives and lime from the many shells which he found, he earned some ready cash. Living was cheap since much of his food came from the wild game that roamed the jungle. Mrs. Carey and Felix recovered, and the boys helped their father build a bamboo and mat house for their home. They also planted a garden. Of these varied activities Carey wrote, "I never felt myself more happy."

The natives, many of whom had deserted this part of the district because of the tigers, flocked back when they saw the missionary's courage. He, in turn, realized in this the possibility of an extended missionary work among them.

"We shall soon have three or four thousand folk near us," he wrote friends in England. "Preachers are needed a thousand times more than people who need preaching. I would not renounce my undertaking for the world."

Into these pleasant circumstances came word that Carey had been mentioned to the government as well-suited for an exploring trip to Assami and Tibet. This appealed to Carey's adventurous spirit. He saw in it not just the possibility to explore the land and to study new plants, but the opportunity to step through an open door to bring the Gospel to these countries.

Before the rumor materialized into a definite appointment, news reached him on March first from Thomas that completely changed all Carey's plans and eventually led him into his real life work in India. Thomas had been given a position as manager of an indigo plantation by a friend, George Udney, who was Commercial Resident at Malda, some three hundred miles distant. Another similar position was open at Mudnabutty about thirty miles to the north, and Thomas had secured this for Carey.

The salary was generous, being about a thousand dollars a year plus a commission upon yearly sales and a house for his family. Carey would not only earn enough for comfortable living but could also save for the translation and publication of the Scriptures, a project dear to his heart. He would have no further need for financial support from the Mission Society at home. He would have a Christian employer and close association again with Thomas. It could be nothing but God's leading. He instantly accepted, though it saddened him to leave his villagers and the agricultural work which had engaged his attention.

On May 23, 1794, the family started on the river journey to Malda, a twenty-three-day trip. Kitty, Mrs. Carey's sister stayed at Debhatta. Mr Short, the kindly host who had succored the Carey family on their arrival, had asked her to marry him. On the following February the two were married.

Carey and his family arrived at Malda on June 15, 1794. On his way he had preached in the vernacular that he might discover his progress in the use of Bengali. He found himself "much at loss for words," as he expressed it. On his first Sunday at Malda he spoke to the Europeans in the home of his host, Mr. Udney. He wrote, "My joy in having my tongue set at liberty again for the Gospel, I can hardly describe."

His environment at the new station was a vast improvement over any he had as yet experienced. The house was a two-story building with spacious rooms and large windows. Surrounding it was sufficient land for a garden, and the landscape stretching beyond was picturesque and inviting — green rice fields, shining pools of water with palm-fringed banks. The natives in their graceful white garments flitted here and there about their tasks, drawing exclamations from the Careys.

William wrote the Mission Society, saying, "A large door is open and I have great hopes. If any lose caste for the sake of the Gospel I can offer them employment." At the same time he entered in his journal, "If, after God has so wonderfully made way for us, I should be negligent, the blackest brand of infamy must lie upon my soul."

His first efforts were turned toward mastering the business which was the source of his support. The peasants brought in great bundles of the indigo plant, which were then steeped and fermented in large vats. Exact judgment was necessary to decide when the green water from the plants must be run into vats below, where it was beaten wildly by the coolies until it changed to blue. Carey soon learned when the water had been stirred sufficiently. The water was then allowed to granulate and settle. Following this, the water was drained off, leaving the indigo dye in the bottom of the vat. The sediment, cleaned, boiled, strained, pressed, dried, packed and cut into cubes was then sent to Calcutta. Carey entered into this work with zest, for the practical use of plants had always been of keen interest to him.

All did not go well with the missionary's family. The season was unhealthy and Carey could scarcely get enough people to carry on the work. He himself felt ill, and his five-year-old son, Peter, a child so gifted that he had already practically mastered Bengali, became sick and passed away. The grief of the family was augmented by the difficulties encountered in making burial arrangements for the little body. Because of religious and caste rules of India neither Hindu nor Mohammedan would assist in the burial rites. No one would make a coffin, nor could any be found to dig a grave or even carry the body. At last a few of the outcasts were persuaded to aid in these sad offices. So fierce became the contention about the matter that Carey, so ill he could scarcely stand, had to interfere to quell a disturbance.

These difficulties and sorrows further affected Dorothy's unsteady mind. The affair was so disastrous to William's health that Udney generously sent him, in the company of Thomas, up the winding river to the border of Bhutan. Here in a somewhat more bracing climate, with the glorious snowy Kinching-umga range in view, and a new world of plant life to investigate and study, Carey was soon restored to normal health. He learned to love the sturdy, kindly Bhutans, and he longed to plant a Christian mission among them.

Had Carey's desire to evangelize the Bhutans been realized a far different story would have been written concerning India. Bhutan, it must be remembered, along with the state of Nepal, is one of the two or three nations of the world left at this time whose doors are not open to Christianity.

When his health had been completely restored Carey returned to his activities at the station. At first he found the Indians rather cool toward him, for the dealings of some of the indigo planters had made them wary. They soon discovered, however, that this English manager was different. He was kind, honest and deeply interested in their welfare — not only physical, but mental and spiritual. His indignation burned at the exploitation of the poor he saw on every side. He recognized the right of underprivileged tenants who had been cheated by the land owners. He was greatly irritated by the way in which the foremen in the indigo works robbed the coolies. The overseers, too, demanded a commission from the workers under them. In his trips throughout the district he became familiar with "every process of local farming, every secret of economy, every trick of the people."

Carey was lonely, however. Thomas and his plant were some eighteen miles away, while Mr. Udney at Malda was thirty miles distant. His wife's mental disorders became suddenly worse. For two years no word from England reached him, his letters in some manner having been miscarried. Of these problems and difficulties he wrote in his journal:

"February 3, 1795. This is, indeed, the Valley of the Shadow of Death to me . . . O, what would I give for a sympathetic friend to whom I might open my heart. But God is here, who not only has compassion but who can save to the uttermost."

Again on March 14, he wrote, "Mine is a lonesome life."

In the midst of this loneliness William Carey, who had anchored his trust in the Rock of Ages, found comfort in the nearness of Christ who sustained him. He little feared the problems that arose. He knew that he was in India under the divine guidance of his Heavenly Father. Whatever the task, however great the strong trials which might force themselves upon him, he knew that God's all-seeing eye was upon him.

To add to his depression, when letters did finally arrive, some of them contained criticisms of his actions from the Home Committee. These criticisms were more or less related to his employment in the indigo business. He and Thomas were "earnestly cautioned and entreated not to engage too deeply in the affairs of this life lest it should dampen their ardor, if not divert them from their work."

This cut Carey to the heart, for from the very beginning of his study and interest in mission work it had been a matter of both good sense and conscience, as far as he could see, that pioneer missionaries should be self-supporting. It had been his aim to become self-sufficient for the mission field. In that way the Home Committee could not force him to return to England. Carey wrote the committee, saying:

"To vindicate my own spirit or conduct I am very averse, it being a maxim with me that if my conduct will not vindicate itself, it is not worth vindicating. We really thought we were acting in conformity with the Society's wish. True, they did not specify indigo; but trade in timbers was suggested, and cultivation of the ground. Whether the spirit of the missionary is swallowed up in the pursuits of the merchant it becomes me not to say. Our labors will speak for us. I may declare that after a bare allowance for my family, my whole income, and some months much more, goes for the purpose of the Gospel, in supporting pundits and schoolteachers and the like. The love of money has not prompted me to this indigo business. I am poor indeed and always shall be till the Bible is published in Bengali and Hindustani, and the people need no further instruction."

Carey's heart was devoted to giving India the Bible in her own tongue, and toward this end he constantly strived. Whenever he was not overseeing the interests of the large indigo factory, or preaching in Bengali to the natives in his humble, feeble manner, he was constantly at the work of translating the Word of God. He continued his own study with Ram Basu. With this native as his instructor he studied Bengali and Hindustani. The necessity of learning to use the immediate dialect of the district in which he was located somewhat delayed his progress, however. He soon decided in order to master most speedily the vernacular dialects, a knowledge of the basic mother tongue, Sanskrit, would be helpful. He noted that Max Muller said:

"The study of Sanskrit and literature is the best means of making any man who is to spend five and twenty years of his life in India, feel at home among Indians, a fellow-worker among them, and not an alien among aliens."

"I am learning the Sanskrit language," he wrote to an English friend, "which with only the helps to be procured here is perhaps the hardest language in the world."

The translation of the Scriptures into the Bengali continued, and by 1797 the New Testament was completed in this language. Some of this translation had been the work of Thomas, since he had begun it long before Carey had joined him. In this language work Carey was to suffer a severe loss, for Ram, the teacher became unfaithful, and with sadness the missionary was forced to dismiss him. Carey became much dejected and wrote Dr. Pearce in the homeland, saying:

"It appears as if all were sunk and gone. For nine years Ram Basu has been teacher and colleague, first of Thomas and then of myself, a scholar of the very best natural ability and a faithful counselor."

Ram Basu had lived with the Careys as a member of the family. They had looked upon him almost as a son. If, after all, he could not remain faithful, what could they hope of other possible converts. His deflection from the right path was a sad blow and had serious consequences. As he was master of the school Carey had established, his dismissal caused it to be closed for lack of a teacher. Carey wrote Andrew Fuller of this double misfortune, saying:

"We are determined to hold on though our discouragement be a thousand times greater. We have the same ground of hope as you in England — the promised power and faithfulness of God."

William Carey was not to be deflected from the aim of his life by the immediate difficulties that beset his path. His eyes were heaven-fixed, his mind was at peace because it was stayed on God. Though storms might arise locally and for the moment beset him, still the missionary knew that he must fight his way through these difficulties to the end of the shining rainbow of success which God had promised him. It was this determination to arrive at the goal that God had placed upon Carey's vision that made him the successful missionary he became.

Side by side with his linguistic study and translating of the Bible went his preaching. He had by this time so mastered the dialect of the people where he was working, that on Sundays and a few evenings during the week he was able to visit the nearby villages and speak to the natives. Often these trips were on foot or on horseback. He sometimes covered half of his district each week.

"Preaching the Gospel," he commented, "is the very element of my soul. Over twenty miles square I publish Christ's name."

The people became interested in the missionary and received his message. Many times he spoke to as many as five hundred during his Sunday sermon. Though they were willing to hear his Gospel, they were not ready to accept his Christ. This did not deter Carey in his determination to proclaim the saving power of the Gospel.

"Never were the people more willing to hear," he reported, "yet more slow to understand. Caste has cut off all motives to inquiry and exertion, and made stupid contentment the habit of their lives. Harmless, indifferent, vacant, they plod on in the path of their forefathers; even truths in geography, economy and other sciences out of the beaten track make no more impression upon them than the sublimer truths of religion."

To help break through this darkness he started a school and planned a college for the training of twelve young boys. They were to be fed, clothed and educated; their studies to include Sanskrit, Persian, the Scriptures, and some of the sciences. At the time, however, this proved to be but a dream.

Indefatigably as Carey worked, little outward fruit appeared. In his six years in this field he had not won a single native convert, despite the seeming interest which the villagers displayed. He had been the means of the conversion of a number of Europeans, but the Indians, although admitting, "It is in our hearts to follow the new teachings," remained aloof. The price was more than they could pay since it meant their being thrown out of caste, or of losing all that they held dear.

Carey was often depressed by this lack of success and blamed himself for it. "O God, make me a true Christian," he often humbly prayed during these hours of distress. Still he would fall back on God's promise to support him. "I have God," he affirmed, "and His Word is true. Whatever effect God has had in stirring me up to the work and wrought wonders to prepare my way, I can trust His promises and be at peace."

After Ram's dismissal Carey begged the people at home to send more helpers to India. John Fountain unexpectedly arrived on October 10, 1796. This greatly strengthened Carey's soul, for the two had much in common. Fountain came from a neighboring English county, near Carey's home county. He had been a choir-boy and was a great lover of music. His funds were limited, but so enthusiastic was he for the work, that he had traveled at steerage rates.

In writing for helpers Carey suggested a plan for their system of living based on his knowledge of the country and his own experience with household expenses. He wrote Andrew Fuller:

"The experiences obtained here I look upon as the very thing which will tend to support the mission. I know now all the methods of agriculture that are in use. I know the lowest rate of housekeeping in this country. I will now propose to you what I would recommend to the Society. (You will find it similar to what the Moravians do. Seven or eight families can be maintained for nearly the same expense as one, if this method be pursued. I then earnestly entreat the Society to set their faces this way and send out more missionaries. We ought to have seven or eight families together. Our families should be considered nurseries for the Mission and among us should be persons capable of teaching school, so as to educate our children).

"I recommend all living together in a number of little straw houses, forming a line or square, and of having nothing of our own but all general stock. One or two should be elected stewards to preside over all the management which should with respect to eating, drinking, worship, learning, preaching, excursions, etc., be reduced to fixed rules."

At the same time Carey was mulling over the problem of how to get the Scriptures printed once he had finished his translations. To secure the necessary printing equipment from England was too costly. Finally he heard of a press in Calcutta that was for sale. Mr. Udney generously presented it to Carey as a gift. When it finally landed at Mudnabutty and the Indians saw Carey's and Fountain's joy and interest in it, they called it "the sahib's idol."

However, an unexpected turn of events upset their plans.

Carey had greatly depended upon Mr. Udney, but at this time he decided to give up his indigo factories and return to England. The recent season had been a bad one. Carey wrote concerning this:

"All my attention is required to repair what I can of the ravages of a very calamitous flood which has just swept away all the year's hopes. About ten days ago, I went all over this neighborhood and the prospects were charming. The fields were covered with rice, hemp, indigo, cucumbers and gourds. On Friday last, I went over the same parts in a boat where not a vestige of anything could be seen. All was a level plain of water from two to twenty feet deep. The rivers have made two large lakes three miles wide and fifty miles long."

The prospect for the following year's crop was no better than for the previous one. A drought had burned up all the fields. Water supplies were also dried up. Only unsanitary puddles were left for drinking. Consequently an epidemic broke out "such as had scarcely ever been known before," Carey said, "six or seven dying weekly in every little village." John Fountain succumbed to its scourge and Carey despaired of his life.

With these difficulties facing the factory owner, he abandoned the indigo enterprise. Carey first considered going to Bhutan (where he had spent several months recuperating from an illness) and starting a mission there. He and Thomas had made a second visit and their delight in these friendly people was greatly increased. Word had recently come from England, however, that helpers were on their way. Carey felt that he must provide a place for them, so instead of going to Bhutan, he took his savings and purchased an indigo factory at Khidurpur, some twelve miles to the north of his present location.

Finally word was received that the party consisting of Joshua Marshman, his wife and two children, Daniel

Burson, William Grant, his wife and two children, a Miss
Tidd, who was coming to marry John Fountain, and William
Ward, had landed on October 5, 1799, at the settlement
of Serampore, on the Hoogly River near Calcutta.

Ward was the printer Carey had met in England.
Speaking of his hope of translating the Bible, Carey had
said to Ward, "You must come and print it for us."

Although the party was in Danish territory, the British
authorities ordered them to return to England as soon as
they learned the newcomers were missionaries. Colonel Bie,
governor of Serampore, however, took up their cause. The
situation was too indefinite, however to continue. Some
decision must be made as to the missionaries' final quarters
and placement. Ward came to Carey to discuss the outlook.
Of this visit Ward wrote:

"Sunday, December 1, 1799. This morning, we left the
boat and walked a mile and a half to Carey's house . . .
Carey is very little changed from what I recollected; rather
stouter and — blessed be God — a young man still. He
lives in a small village, in a large brick house — two storied
— with Venetian windows and mat doors. Fountain lives
in a bungalow a quarter of a mile away. Mrs. Carey is
wholly deranged. Their four boys talk Bengali fluently.
Felix is fourteen or fifteen. There is a mission school of
about thirty."

Carey was still at Mudnabutty, not having yet moved to
his new indigo factory. He listened thoughtfully to all
Ward told him. Grant had already died of fever at Serampore, leaving his wife and two children. The British authorities would not permit the missionaries to enter the
territory of the East India Company. Serampore on the
other hand, would welcome them and permit them to preach,
establish schools and print the Scriptures in the native
language. The prospects were tempting to Carey, for he
recognized this as an opening for the complete work he

longed to do, but it meant the loss of all he had invested in the indigo factory.

"It was all so affecting to my mind," he wrote to Fuller at this time, "that I scarcely remember having felt more deeply on any occasion whatsoever. No one could gage the conflict of this trial but myself." The following morning Carey and Ward reached a decision. Ward said concerning it, "Monday, December 2. Carey has made up his mind to leave all and follow our Saviour to Serampore."

God's hand was in the move. Udney's successor as the Commercial Resident of Malda was opposed to missions and would have hampered mission work anywhere in the district. He would not have permitted Carey's village evangelization program, nor would he have tolerated the printing of the Gospel in the native languages. Furthermore, a new ruling of the government prohibited the use or location of any printing press in Bengal outside of Calcutta. Thus, the printing of the Scriptures even at Khidurpur would not have been possible. Years later Carey wrote of this providential move saying:

"Not till we could choose no longer, and even then with the utmost reluctance, did we bring ourselves to relinquish what we had begun in Mudnabutty. We only painfully complied with dire necessity. But now we see that the Divine Hand was in it, and are convinced that this is the very place where we ought and are best advantaged to be."

Seemingly Carey's work at Mudnabutty had reached its end. For six years he had labored there faithfully. In his personal contact with the people, he had won their confidence and their love. Through his kindness and fair dealings he had given them a better and different idea of the English overlord than had been theirs from contacts with his predecessors. William had done much to help the sick, for he had become a successful pupil of Thomas in the field of medicine. He recognized that he must not only be able to heal the souls of the Indians with the Gospel, but to touch the sick bodies as well.

However, he was greatly perturbed by his lack of an Indian convert. He laid the difficulty to his own short-comings. Among the Europeans of the district, he had made good progress, having touched or influenced many of the officials. These men had helped him in his work by con-tributing money and aiding in the establishment of schools. Carey felt that with the planting of this seed the work surely would grow. He determined that, convert or no, he would spread the Gospel by preaching and translating the Scrip-ture.

An important part of Carey's labor was not generally known. He had quietly continued the work of translating the Scriptures into the native language and finally completed the task. The entire Bible, except for a few Old Testament chapters, was ready for publication in Bengali. Both Fountain and Thomas had assisted in this almost super-human task, but the bulk of the work was Carey's. Thou-sands of sheets in his neat penmanship awaited a printer. Carey was hungering to see this come rolling from the press ready for distribution among the Indians. Serampore was the open door for this publication to be accomplished. Little wonder then that the loss of money at Khidurpur did not greatly trouble him.

On January 1, 1800, with his own and Fountain's goods, the printing press, a collection of plants for Serampore which had been given him by a friend, Dr. Roxburgh, manager of Calcutta's Botanical Gardens, Carey and his party boarded a boat at Malda for the river trip to the new field. There he intended to conduct the work along the plan he had suggested to the Society — a communal mission settlement of which Carey was to be leader and manager.

From a shoemaker's bench in a little English village, where he had educated himself, Carey had finally reached

faraway Bengal. He had almost starved in a tumbledown
house in Calcutta. He had lived in the jungles of Sunderbunds. To preach the Gospel to poor peasants, he had become an indigo planter. Now he was to settle amid a dense
population, to found a movement the fruit of which is
still being garnered. God had been his divine sustenance
and support.

To the core of his being, Carey was a missionary.
So broad was his attack upon the problems of penetrating
and becoming a part of India's life that he would not be
deterred. The Commander of his soul had challenged him
with these words, "Go . . . preach the Gospel." William
Carey had recognized this call to the evangelization of
India as a personal responsibility and obligation which
rested upon his own soul.

With several years of missionary struggle back of him,
Carey had completed one task which he had set as an
objective of his Indian labors — translating the Bible into
the Bengali. He was ready now to attack the problems of
winning converts among the Indians to the Man of Galilee,
whose command he had accepted, whose challenge stirred
his soul.

Chapter 5

THE FIRST HINDU CONVERT

Serampore proved to be a veritable city of refuge for
the missionaries who arrived at this Danish-Chinese settlement on January 10, 1800. The city was under the protection of the Danish government, with its executive control in the hands of Colonel Bie. The British authorities
did not interfere with the Danish settlement. Happily by
this time there were various foreign settlements dotting
the free ports of China, and among these Serampore was
outstanding. God's approval was upon the move which
Carey and his compatriots made.

The city was in the heart of a populous district only two
hours from Calcutta, with the world's commerce passing its
doors. The harbor and the docks were crowded with the
ships of many countries. The population was polyglot.
Across the river was Barrackpore, a resort and military
station to which the Governor-General of India and the
fashionable and wealthy of Calcutta flocked for week-end
parties and similar gaieties. Governor Bie brought visitors
from many distant places to the mission service.

In this way news of the work Carey was doing was borne
far and near. No better site could have been chosen for the
establishment of the enterprise Carey envisioned. It was
a center from which the Gospel could be carried to all
points in the East. Truly this was the leading of God.

The city itself was attractive. Carey described it as,

"populous, well-ordered, healthful, and a beautiful town."
Others writing of it, said, "Serampore is a handsome place,
kept beautifully clean, and looking more like a European
town than Calcutta or any of its neighboring cantonments.
On the banks of the river the air is pleasant and healthful.
The scene is enlivened by the plying up and down of numerous boats."

Carey, Marshman and Ward were leaders in the mission
work. Marshman's background is indeed interesting. His
home had furnished little educational opportunity. He had
been so eager for knowledge as a boy, however, that by
the time he was twelve he had read all the books he could
borrow — more than a hundred. Among them were *Jose-
phus*, Milton's *Paradise Lost*, Voltaire's *Candidus* and others
of a similar nature. At fifteen he went to London. There
his love for books led him to get a job as a book seller.
This proved to be tedious and humdrum, however. Once
when on an errand to deliver some volumes, Marshman was
so overcome by depression and discouragement that he sat
down and wept.

Finally he returned to his native village where he renewed his religious associations and became a local
preacher. He married Hannah Shepherd in 1791, and at
the same time engaged in studies to prepare for the
ministry. Here he met Dr. Ryland, who told him of the
missionary work in which Carey was engaged. Marshman
immediately decided to devote his attention and life to such
an endeavor. In later years he became the father-in-law of
General Havelock, who has often been called "the saviour
of India." In a religious sense Marshman himself could lay
claim to part of the honor of this title. Carey said of him:

"Marshman is all keenness for God's work. Often have
I seen him eye a group of persons like a hawk and go up
to try on them the Gospel's utmost strength. I have known
him to engage with such for hours. It has filled me with

shame . . . he is a prodigy of diligence and prudence. Learning the language is mere play for him. He has acquired in four months as much as I did in eight."

Marshman's wife Hannah, who took up the management of communal household affairs, was particularly fitted for this task. For forty-six years she fulfilled her duties with "extraordinary prudence, devoutness and zeal," as Carey remarked. "She not only attended to the purely domestic affairs, but helped in the schools, and the church work. She devoted much time to the homes not only of the native Christian families, but what was unusual at the time, she engaged likewise in friendly ministrations among the Hindu families whose doors were rapidly opened to her. Her wide range of activities shows not only her ability, but a personality that admitted her to communities not always open to the foreigners."

Ward, as has been noted, was a printer. Indeed, when God put it in his heart to sail for India, Ward became for Carey one of his greatest assistants, because Carey, as time was to show, was supremely a writer, whose finished products must be given to India by means of the printed page. It was in the field of printing that Ward was outstanding. He became interested in missionary work after having met Carey in the homeland. Later, he offered his services to the Committee and was accepted on October 16, 1798. He wrote to Carey at this time, saying:

"Sometime in the spring I hope to embark with others. It is in my heart to live and die with you."

With such zeal for the work there is little wonder that he proved so faithful a laborer in the vineyard. Carey said of him:

"Brother Ward is the very man we want. He enters into the work with his whole soul. I have much pleasure in him and expect much of him."

The others of the party, Grant and Burson, soon passed away. Fountain's widow later married Mr. Ward. Dr. Thomas was engaged elsewhere for the time, so Carey, Marshman and Ward thus became the valuable mission workers. Thomas said of them, "Three such men as Carey, Marshman and Ward, so suited to one another in their work, are not to be found I think in the whole world."

Writing concerning this happy group of missionaries, Richter notes: "The three at Serampore were of that type of self-made men so often to be met with in English history, men of insatiable appetite for learning, and of practical ability, dismayed by no difficulties and boundless in industry and patience. Carey especially was a man of heroic diligence. Each acted as a complement to the others so perfectly and harmoniously that their living together tripled their work power. They had one household in common in Serampore until death, and stood by one another inseparably in weal and woe, during years of severe trial."

The three planned the work with sound common sense. To them the breaking of the hard shell which enveloped India was a serious task to be accomplished by sincere devotion on their part to the work at hand; by all the artifices which their native ability and training afforded; and by serious, hard labor. Sir J. W. Kays writes:

"Never have men addressed themselves to the holy work of evangelization in a purer spirit nor with more earnestness of purpose; and yet at the same time with sounder, good, practical sense and steadier perseverance in the adaptation of all legitimate means to the great end they set before them. They expected no miracles to be wrought in their behalf. They knew that much toil was necessary for even scanty success, and they never spared themselves."

A Moravian mission had been located in Serampore before and had failed. The new trio of missionaries did not wish to repeat their predecessor's mistake. They realized they were blazing a new trail in mission work, not only in locating their mission in an overwhelmingly Hindu community with strong Brahmin influences, but also in their plan of community living. They took up the task with confidence, however, even though they realized its serious hazards. Ward wrote concerning this endeavor: "I tremble almost before we begin to live together. So much depends on a man's disinterestedness, forbearance, meekness and self denial . . . Much wisdom will be needed . . . only few are fit to live in such a settlement as ours is to be, where selfish passions must be crushed and the love of Christ swallow up all else."

They went courageously forward. Ward gives details. He says:

"The renting of a house or houses would ruin us. We hoped therefore to have been able to purchase land and build mat houses, but we can get none properly situated. We have in consequence purchased of the Governor's nephew a large house in the middle of the town . . . it consists of a spacious verandah and hall with two rooms on each side. Rather more to the front are two other rooms separate, and on one side is a storehouse, separate also, which will make a printing office. It stands by the riverside upon a pretty large piece of ground."

In time the influence of the missionary settlement was felt throughout the Oriental world. Carey soon beautified the grounds with botanical growth. He surrounded the house with mahogany trees, and the avenue under them became known as "Carey's Walk."

Ward gives further details of their living conditions under the date of January 18, 1800. He writes:

"About six o'clock we rise; brother Carey to his garden; brother Marshman to his school at seven; Felix and I to the printing office. At eight, the bell rings for family worship. We assemble in the hall, sing, read and pray. Breakfast. Afterwards, brother Carey goes to the translation, or reading proof; brother Marshman to school, and the rest to the printing office . . . We print three half sheets of 2000 each in a week . . . At twelve o'clock we take a luncheon; then most of us shave and bathe, read and sleep before dinner which we have at three. After dinner we deliver our thoughts on a text or question; this we find to be very profitable. Brother and sister Marshman keep their schools till after two. In the afternoon, if business be done in the office, I read and try to talk Bengali with the Brahmin. We drink tea about seven, and have little or no supper.

"We have Bengali preaching once or twice in the week, and on Thursday evening we have an experience meeting. On Saturday evening, we meet to compare differences and transact business, after prayers, which is always immediately after tea."

The success of this type of family living no doubt was due to Carey's plan of equality for all, pre-eminence for none, not even for himself, though no doubt he would have been well received as leader in the venture. Carey insisted upon rule by majority, the allocation of activities and duties by rotation of work, even to the purchasing of supplies, presidency at the table, bookkeeping, management of servants, the interviewing of callers, and the conduct of the weekly services in English. He would have no man called master save one, Jesus Christ.

Students soon began to come to the school, for the wealthy among the English were only too glad to find such a place of high instruction for their children. It soon became a slogan that "everyone sends his son to Serampore." Fees from this school and profits from the printing press quickly put the party on a self-supporting basis.

Thursday, April 24, 1800, was celebrated as Thanksgiving Day for the completion of their building. Carey looked upon this as an accomplishment carried to fruition only through the blessings and mercies of God. Appropriate services were held, and an address was written which was to be sent to Governor Bie. In return, to show his appreciation of the work of the missionaries, the Governor sent a note to Andrew Fuller, saying:

"I am happy in possessing these, as I shall be if their number increases. This world yields plenty of mold whereof earthen vessels are made, little dust that gold cometh from."

Thus the Governor expressed his evaluation of the services and character of the missionaries. He recognized the growing reputation which was attaching itself to the work of Carey and his associates. The printing presses especially were well-received by him. Equally important in his eyes was the school which he recognized as playing a vital part in training the English and foreign youth to labor in India.

In May of 1800 Ward's presses gave to the world the first leaf of Carey's New Testament in Bengali an achievement toward which Carey had directed his concerted efforts for many years. Carey the cobbler, now became Carey the scholar. In the annals of Christian sacrifice and achievement there are few to equal this translating task which Carey took upon himself. He recognized himself not as a genius but as a plodder — a man whose native abilities had been heightened by contact with, and by the direction of the Holy Spirit.

At the same time John Thomas surprised the missionary party with a visit. While Thomas' influence in India might have been insignificant, due to his many personal failings and to the fact that he was constantly in debt, still it must be remembered that it was Thomas who sparked into life the embers of desire in Carey's heart to bring the Gospel into India. He must always stand in missionary history as the man who inspired William Carey to attempt the work to which he devoted his entire life.

There was, however, a perturbing element in the mission work at this beautiful location. It seemed that the blessing of God had been in an unusual way upon the labors of Carey and his associates. God had given them spacious grounds and supplied such buildings as were necessary. He had inclined the hearts of the foreign element in Serampore and neighboring cities to send their children to the mission school. Carey had, with God's leading, placed the venture upon a sound financial footing, and now the blessings of heaven had attended the issuing of the first pages of the Gospel in Bengali. But here, as before, there were no native converts.

Carey recognized that he had come to India not to build schools, not to print circulars, but to transform the nation by winning converts to Jesus Christ. He threw himself with all his spiritual intensity, mental ardor and physical endowment into preaching the Gospel. He wrote many leaflets which Ward's presses gave to India. Many listened attentively to Carey's sermons, but they waited to see what the Brahmin would do. The Brahmin as a rule were opposed to the new teaching which Carey gave them.

They were surprised at Carey's knowledge of their own sacred writings, and often these Brahmin as high caste leaders of the nation debated with Carey upon the subjects of the Gospel. But none ever stepped across the line to become Christians. William Carey tried satire on them and cleverly showed them the powerlessness of their own gods, yet this failed. He endeavored to preach the Gospel directly to them, still they refused to accept his Christ. Finally, Carey decided to center his message in the wonderful story of Christ's love and His supreme sacrifice to win the world to Himself, especially the Brahmin. But though they were touched and often wept, still they took no definite step. Writing under the date of July 27, 1800, Ward said:

"We are often much disheartened, though we try to keep up each other's spirits. At present, it is a dead calm; not one whisper, 'What shall I do to be saved?' "

Even Carey himself in October, 1800, wrote to John Williams, Baptist minister in New York:

"No people can have more surrendered their reason. In business they are not deficient, but in religion they seem without understanding. But a people can hardly be better than their gods. They have made themselves idols after their own hearts. Hindus have not the fierceness of American Indians, but this is abundantly made up for by cunning and deceit. Moral rectitude makes no part of their religious system; no wonder, therefore, they are immersed in iniquity."

To another mission worker he wrote:

"Never was such a combination of false principles as here. In other heathen lands, conscience may often be appealed to with effect. Here God's law is erased and idolatrous ceremony is engraven in its stead. All are bound to their present state by caste. To break the chains of caste a man must endure to be renounced and abhorred by his wife, children and friends. Every tie that twines around the heart of a husband, father and neighbor must be torn and broken, ere a man can give himself to Christ."

After Carey had done all in his power to present the Gospel of Jesus Christ, he recognized the problems which a decision to stand firmly on the Christian side must present to the natives. Facing these facts seriously, he concluded thus:

"I have no doubt but that God will establish His name in this country. Our labors may be only those of pioneers, but Truth will certainly prevail and this kingdom among the others be the salvation of our God."

This vision of success proved prophetic, for it was shortly thereafter that the "dead calm" the missionaries' work experienced was at last swept away. Thomas had brought with him a native workman named Sakira, who had become interested in Thomas' preaching and had stayed on at his factory at lower wages so that he might have an opportunity to learn more of the Gospel of Christ.

On Tuesday, November 25, 1800, he came before the members of the mission staff and told them that he had accepted Christ as his personal Saviour and asked to be baptized.

The missionaries were so overjoyed at this — the first fruit of their Indian labors — that they sprang to their feet and sang the Doxology. Sakira asked permission to return home that he might bring his motherless child to the station. This permission was granted, and the baptism was fixed for the Sunday after his return. Strangely enough, however, he never came back to the mission. Whether his courage deserted him, or he was murdered by his friends because of the decision to become a Christian, will never be known. Often the first converts in India and among other foreign people were murdered so that the effects of the new Gospel might be stamped out.

Sakira's failure to return was a great disappointment to Carey. It did show him, however, that the Spirit of God was working even in the dark confines of India. God soon was to give Carey and his fellow-workers the first convert. Again it was Thomas who became the human instrument that started the chain of events which produced this convert.

Krishna Pal, an Indian youth, had heard of Christianity through the Moravian missionaries. Later, he had met

Thomas who told him of the Mission School at Serampore.
Krishna Pal was now a teacher of the Mantras, but he could
not destroy the memory of his early contacts with Christianity. Often he talked with Dr. Thomas and his interest
in Christ and the Gospel was revived. He lived near Thomas
and when he dislocated his shoulder he sent to this English
friend for help.

Carey and Marshman went with Thomas, and they told the
Hindu youth about Christ and the power of the Gospel to
transform a life. The next day Krishna Pal came to the
Mission for further treatment, and after that he returned for
daily Christian instruction. He passed on what the missionaries told him to his wife, Rasamayi, to his sister, Jaymani,
and a friend, Gokul.

On December 22, 1800, both he and Gokul accepted
Christ. That day they ate with the missionaries — a supreme sacrifice on their part — for thereby they as Hindus
broke caste. Henceforth they became as outcasts from those
of their own caste. In the evening the two women joined
with the men, and the following Sunday was set by the missionaries as the time for the first Christian baptism.

Rioting broke out among the Hindus when the news
was spread. The mob hailed Krishna before the Governor,
but Colonel Bie forbade them to harm him and set a guard
for his protection. Already the mob had snatched his
eldest little girl from the home. The crowd threatened,
taunted, jeered and said that if the baptism took place
they would tear the Christians limb from limb. But Krishna
Pal stood firm, for Jesus Christ had entered into his life
and enabled him to face these storms.

When the day arrived Krishna Pal, along with Carey's
son Felix, was baptized. The ceremoney took place at the
riverside opposite the Mission's gates. The Governor, a
number of Europeans, as well as a sprinkling of Hindus
and Mohammedans, were present, for this was an affair

that had aroused much interest. The scene was impressive. To those who glimpsed beneath the surface the meaning was significant.

"The conversion and transformation of one Hindu," Marshman said of the event, "was like a decisive experiment in natural history of universal application. The divine grace that changed one Indian's heart could obviously change a hundred thousand."

Thus the first fruits of Carey's mission work were granted to him by the gracious anointing of God. Shortly thereafter Krishna Pal's wife, his sister Jaymani, together with Gokul and his entire family were baptized. A widow, who became the first in Bengal of this unfortunate and pitiable class to know the freedom, mercy and comfort of the Gospel of Christ, was also baptized with them.

March 5, 1801, became another day of supreme joy at the mission, for on that date the first bound Bengali New Testament was placed on the Communion Table. It was the first book for the people ever printed in Bengal's native language, and it represented seven and one-half years of Carey's life. It was a triumph for his perseverance and a just reward for his scholarship. It proved once and for all to the world that application to the dead languages of the past would pay rich dividends for any youth who would dare devote himself to mastering them with supreme concentration.

"March 5. This evening we had thanksgiving," Ward entered in his diary, "for the finishing of the New Testament. Carey spoke in English and Bengali and the rest of us prayed. A comfortable meeting."

Not only was that a "comfortable meeting," but it was also a supreme event in the history of Christian missions, a day to be remembered in the triumphal march of the Gospel of Jesus Christ through the centuries. Many other translations were to follow. This was but the first fruits of Carey's linguistic labors. Following his example, multiplied hundreds of new translations have been given to the various peoples of the world in their own language. Today the Gospel has been given in whole or part to the world in more than eleven hundred languages and dialects. Truly Carey can be looked upon as one of the fathers of this great movement to give the Gospel to all the tribes of the world in their own languages and dialects.

It was right that in that "comfortable meeting" of which Ward spoke, Carey and his missionary friends were joined by the new Indian converts, the fruits of their Gospel labors. While the group of converts was small, after these long years of Christian effort, still they were the foreshadowing of the success which was to mark Carey's endeavors in India.

A hundred copies of this Bengali New Testament were sent to Dr. Ryland, in the homeland. One of these went to the Earl of Spencer, who at the time was making a collection of Bibles. The Earl personally congratulated Carey's father and sent $250.00 to Serampore to help carry forward the translation of the Old Testament. He also suggested that a copy of the Testament be sent at his request to the King. This was done, and in turn the King acknowledged the Testament by saying, "I am greatly pleased that any of my subjects should be employed in this manner." A copy was also presented to the King of Denmark, for it was a Danish settlement which had afforded refuge for Carey and his co-laborers when England and the East India Company would have returned them to their native land.

This Bengali New Testament was "the first stroke of the axe levelled at the banyan tree of India's superstition."

A helpful addition to the workers who were hewing down these heathen beliefs was found in Krishna Pal, who knew these superstitions and rites as only a Hindu could. He accompanied the missionaries on their preaching trips, and though he was evicted by his Brahman landlord (the land was taken from him though he had partially paid for it) he never faltered. The gossip and comment he had aroused among the Hindus turned the attention of many to the Christian teaching with more earnestness than the persuasion of the missionaries could have done. Some of the higher castes became interested and the number of inquirers grew. God thus was in the persecution which was heaped upon Krishna Pal and used it to further the work of the Kingdom.

Sadness soon crept into this tidal wave of rejoicing, however. The excitement and joy of the conversions and baptism were too much for Thomas' nervous temperament. His mind became unbalanced and the day of Krishna Pal's baptism he had to be forcibly restrained in one of the buildings of the Mission. Mrs. Carey likewise was affected and had to be locked in her room. While these were heavy burdens to be borne, still the mission staff shouldered them. A debt of gratitude must ever be paid to the memory of Dr. Thomas, for it was he who first interested Carey and his Mission Society brethren in the work of India.

In the midst of these glad yet sad days a message arrived April 8, 1801, that threw the little colony into a turmoil of excitement. Carey was asked if he would accept an appointment to the staff of Fort William College. This was recognition indeed for a missionary, a Non-Conformist at that, to be offered a post in the heart of the East India Company's territory. It showed more than anything else the place his work had made for him among the influential Englishmen of Calcutta. It was a further step in the leadership of God which in the end was to make of Carey the greatest man of his generation, either in England or in India.

The college had recently been founded by Lord Wellesley, Governor-General of India. He realized that the young clerks of the East India Company who came out from England were not sufficiently educated for the work that lay ahead of them.

Dr. Susil Kumar De, of the Calcutta University wrote in 1800:

"The Company's civil servants, though they produced a few of first-rate ability, had sunk into lowest depths of ignorance and vice. Lads of fifteen to eighteen years were being sent out to India, before their education could be finished, with no opportunity or inducement on their arrival to complete it. At the close of three or four years' residence, the young civilians, endowed with an affluent income and unchecked authority, had not only lost the fruits of their English studies and had gained no useful knowledge of Asiatic literature of business, but were abandoned to pursue their own inclination without guidance or control."

Carey himself doubted his ability to fulfil the duties of the position. He recognized that he himself was self-taught, that he had sat on the benches of no famed university, and that his instruction in languages had been only what he had gleaned through the varied assistance of numerous friends.

"I am almost sunk under the prospect," he wrote to his friend Dr. Ryland, "having never known college discipline. My ignorance of the ways of conducting collegiate exercises is a great weight on my mind." At length he consented, however, "though with fear and trembling." He and his fellow-workers, having the welfare of the Mission foremost in their thoughts, agreed that since the position came unsought, it might be of essential service to the work of the kingdom, and the results should be left to God.

Dubious as Carey was of his own ability, and of practical training, it is doubtful if a better man could have been selected for the task. Carey's character was remarkable for integrity and conscientiousness. His path to learning had been a difficult one. His mind was quick. He was resourceful in his endeavors, and he had mastered the study of human nature. He had a passionate love for learning, and especially was he supremely devoted to the study of languages. He had been appointed as Professor of Bengali, a task which when considered in itself seemed beyond his ability.

God had honored William Carey's services by this appointment. Carey had already shown to the world the worth of his own ability, for had he not given the world the first Bengali New Testament? This alone was recognized as a supreme achievement which qualified him to teach the language to students. Recognizing God's guiding and thinking of the conquest which missions must make in India's soul, Carey entered upon his new task.

Chapter 6

GLORY AMID THE SHADOWS

ONCE CAREY had determined that the teaching position was God's will, he threw himself into this task with all the determination of his character. Never one to be content with half-hearted achievements, the cobbler now became the learned professor. His achievements during this period mark him as one of the most intellectual men of his century. Few have invested their mentality either in the secular or the Christian world with greater visible accomplishments than Carey. At heart a linguist, Carey now had a field wherein he could give full play to the varied range of his literary qualification. What he had learned he had thoroughly mastered by his own initiative.

When called to this professorship, his achievements in the Bengali language were the result of the tutelage of the natives with whom he studied and talked constantly. The great problem of breaking down Indian indifference and prejudice could be successful only through an effective appeal to the intellectuals of the nation. Carey consequently was used of God in a marvelous manner to influence the upper class of people in India. His position in the new college was offered him directly by the Governor-General himself. Carey was successful in reaching the higher strata of the nation only because of the fact that he was a linguistic genius.

The college opened with about one hundred students,

who came mainly from Calcutta, Bombay and Madras. The curriculum included law, political economy, history, geography, mathematics, the classics, with a sprinkling of modern European languages. There were also courses in the history of India, and some in sciences. An important part of the study for these young clerks was the Indian languages. It must be remembered there are numerous languages and dialects spoken freely throughout the great breadth of India. The languages were emphasized so that the clerks of the East India Company, and other government offices could learn them and be able to converse with co-workers in whatever part of the nation they were located. The course of study covered a three-year period.

Since only a member of the Church of England could become a full professor in a government college, Carey was given the title of "tutor." His salary was set at $175 a month, with rooms in Calcutta furnished for the first four years, and his meals at the faculty table in the dormitory. At first he held classes two days a week. Later a third day was added. Usually he made the eighteen-mile journey down the winding Hoogly River to Calcutta on Monday evenings just as the sun was setting, and he made his return trip back to Serampore on Fridays.

These trips were a delight to Carey's adventurous nature. In spirit he became a boy again, re-living those wild scenes envisioned under the spell of his Canadian uncle's tales and descriptions of the New World. The sunsets, brilliant as only India's sunsets could be, appealed to his nature-loving spirit. He enjoyed the luxurious vegetation of the river bank and the ever-changing view of life along the rivers.

Carey chose scholarly Hindus as assistants, among them Ram Basu, for Carey knew the man had unquestionable ability in linguistics. Although Carey was appointed to teach Bengali, he soon added Sanskrit and Marathi to his courses. A need for vernacular textbooks was immediately felt. Carey and his associates set themselves to the task of writing them. From these first efforts came a grammar in the Bengali, as well as Bengali translations from the Sanskrit and various sacred writings of the Hindus. Carey also published *"Colloquies,* which were lively pictures of the manners and notions of the people of Bengali," according to Professor Wilson of Oxford University.

In 1806 Carey became a member of the Asiatic Society, bringing about even greater contact with the intellectual Europeans in India. This society was particularly interested in the literature of the East. Carey unfolded to them a plan for publishing the Indian classics at Ward's Press, located in Serampore. Word of this project was sent to the learned societies of Europe, and the great task was begun.

Dr. Susil Kumar, in his *History of Bengali Literature* said:

"Carey was the center of the learned Bengalis, whom his zeal attracted around him. The impetus which he gave to Bengali learning is to be measured not merely by his productions and his educational labors, but by the influence he exerted and the example he set."

Ram Komal Sen, Secretary of the Asiatic Society wrote:

"I must acknowledge that whatever has been done towards the revival of the Bengali language and its improvement must be attributed to Dr. Carey and his colleagues."

In 1806 Carey was given the full title of Professor and his salary was raised to $7500 yearly. He remained in this high position for approximately thirty years. After seventeen years he was the only member of the faculty who had been there since the founding of the college. His rooms became the center of literary activity, for he drew about him the best minds of the period, from among both the English and the Indians — men who were anxious to further their knowledge and appreciation of India's long history.

Through Carey's efforts grammars were produced in Bengali, Marathi, Punjabi, Telegu and Kanarese. This greatly promoted the study of these various linguistic families which had sprung from the root of the Indian language.

Similarly Carey compiled dictionaries in Bengali, Marathi and the Sanskrit. Professor Wilson of Oxford has said of Carey's work in this realm:

"Local terms are here rendered with the correctness which Carey's knowledge of the peoples' manners and his long domestication among them enabled him to attain; and his scientific acquirements and familiarity with natural history qualified him to employ, and not infrequently to devise characteristic terms for the animal and vegetable products of the East."

This literary work was not confined to mere textbooks. Carey and those who assisted him produced translations from the Sanskrit. They wrote stories, fables, essays, constructed works on law, wove the historical facts of the nation into a literature. In fact they produced a variety of literary material that pictured the whole life and culture of India. "A View of the History, Literature and Religion of the Hindus, with Translations from Their Principal Writings," which was produced by the printer Ward, became an authority on the subject for a half century. In fact, so great was the respect for the accuracy and literary standards of Carey and his colleague Ward, that little if anything was published by the government in the vernaculars and Sanskrit without the missionary's direct approval.

In this way God enabled William Carey's influence gradually to reach out as long fingers of intellectual power touching the various elements of the nation. While this was not direct missionary work in the accepted sense, still, without it, Carey's later achievements would have been impossible.

Many of Carey's students later entered places of great prominence in legal, governmental and financial circles of the nation, indicative of the renown Carey enjoyed and the high quality of his teaching.

Carey himself had attained such an intellectual eminence in the nations, among both the Indians and the government officials, that he was invited to make an address in Sanskrit September 20, 1804, before Lord Wellesley, his brother (the future Duke of Wellington), the judges of the Supreme Court, the city's Council, diplomats and the intellectuals of Calcutta. This was the first speech in Sanskrit ever to be delivered by a European. When Carey spoke to the government of India, the supreme rulers of the nation, as well as the highest officials and leaders, both in intellectual and social circles, were present. Carey's speech read in part:

"The institution of this College will help to break down the barrier of our ignorance of India's languages which has long opposed the influence of our principles and laws and has despoiled our Administration of its energy and effect. 'Sanskrit learning,' say the Brahmin, 'is an extensive forest abounding in varied and beautiful foliage, in flowers and delicate fruits.' But it has hitherto been surrounded by a thick and thorny fence. Scholars like Sir William Jones and Charles Wilkins have here and there broken the fence. This College by the wisdom of Lord Wellesley will make a highway through the wood."

In his wildest dreams while working at his cobbler's bench Carey had never envisioned such a scene. The depth of thought represented in his address shows the magnitude of the mind struggling for expression so many years before in the little English village. Carey realized that it was only by the direct beneficence of God that he had attained his present position. He had set out to be a missionary in whatever sphere God would locate his labors.

Now he found himself delivering an address in Sanskrit before the lords of the Indian nation! When he was finished and sat down, his audience was thrilled and enthralled at the glorious eloquence of his use of the Sanskrit tongue.

"I am very pleased with Mr. Carey's truly original and excellent speech," said the Governor-General. "I esteem a testimony from such a man a greater honor than the applause of courts and parliament."

Some nine months after Carey had taken up his work at the college, Lord Wellesley commissioned him to look into the religious murders of the Hindus, especially the tragic practice of throwing babies into the Ganges River during the annual festival at the Island of Saugor where the Hoogly branch of the Ganges pours into the sea. This investigation was a work close to Carey's heart. His report after thorough investigation resulted in the official banning of the practice.

Later, he initiated research on the Indian practice of widow-burning. He found much to his horror that almost five hundred wives had been burned alive on their husbands' funeral pyres in the immediate vicinity of Calcutta alone. Many of these were mere children, married at an early age. Lord Wellesley's authority was not strong enough to abolish this custom, much to Carey's disappointment. Until it was made illegal Carey never ceased to fight it, however. The practice was totally abolished decades later, a tribute to William Carey's ceaseless struggle against it.

Busy as he was with his teaching, William Carey could not neglect the missionary work so dear to his heart. The first year he worked mostly among his students and civil service associates. The missionary activities in Serampore were advancing steadily under his Serampore colleagues. Especially was the Hindu convert Krishna Pal being blessed in the task of spreading the Gospel. Though his stand for Christianity caused him much trouble and criti-

cism, Krishna remained firm in his declaration of faith.
He built a little shed near his home in which to preach, and
here Carey, too, often spoke on his week-end sojourns.
Krishna gathered in the children and taught them. Gradually this became a rallying place for the Christian
Indians. Krishna's wife and sister assisted in the task, as
also did the Gokuls. The love, gentleness and kindness
of these Christian natives drew others like a powerful mag-
net. The natives could talk freely to Krishna, Gokul and
their families when they might feel a little shy with the
white missionaries, and thus the truth spread far and near.
Krishna started a little school which in time became the
nucleus for a free school for Hindu children.

A decided forward step in the missionary campaign
was the increased interest of the higher castes, for one of
the sneering taunts had been, "Have any Brahmin or
Kyasts believed?" The Kyasts, who were the writer class,
were now represented by one convert, for on New Year's
day, 1802, Carey baptized one of them, and wrote joyfully
of the event:

"I trust a spark is struck which will never be extinguished. The fire is kindled for which Christ expressed
a strong desire."

Others came, among whom was a Brahman "of the
purest and most favored blood." He said, "I love to get
other Brahmin under Carey's knockdown blows." This
high-caste man gave his son Christian teaching, and himself became a teacher in the free school, creating a tremendous stir among the Hindus. Often they cried, "Will
Krishna Pal destroy the caste of us all? Is this highest
caste Brahman to be an outcast?"

The missionaries were jubilant at these glorious results.
Carey wrote, "God is laying the foundation of His temple
in India." Ward later added, "God is famishing the

thoughts of the country and making His own name glorious." They were reaping the rewards for the long and diligent service they had rendered — the answer to their fervent prayers.

In 1802 Carey wrote to the missionary John Williams: "What hath God wrought! Eighteen months ago, we should have been in raptures to have seen one Hindu eat with us. Now, it is sometimes difficult to find room for all who come. Nine Hindus have been baptized, of whom seven walk so as to be an honor to the Gospel. We expect to baptize a Mussleman and another Hindu."

This, however, does not mean there was no opposition, for there was considerable difficulty even among the new recruits themselves. Traders refused to have dealings with them, barbers would not shave them. They were recognized as outcasts or "unclean." Anyone having anything to do with them polluted himself thereby. The opposition in some cases was more serious. Some were murdered for their faith. Others were decoyed to the home of relatives and disappeared forever, their fate unknown. One was drugged and his mind affected. Another convert was so severely flogged by his irate friends that he recanted and turned his back upon Christ. Thus the persecutions went on. But as martyrdom is the rich soil in which Christianity flourishes, the stream of inquirers increased rather than diminished.

William Carey recognized that a price must be paid for these successes. The dark hours of testing and persecution were now arising.

Another problem was found in the deflections here and there among the converts themselves. They were only human and their whole experience had been in an environment wholly different from what is Christian. It is little wonder that some of them fell. Even Krishna Pal and his family had to be rebuked for hardness over varying matters, quarreling among themselves, gossiping and tale-bearing — rebukes that were administered in Christian love and sympathy. Sometimes there arose even actual physical assault among the converts as temper ran high over some misunderstanding or fancied slight.

"How discouraged we sometimes get," said Ward, in these hours of darkness, "by their accusations, quarrels and apparent untruths. Truly a missionary's hardest work is not travel in a hot clime."

After one outburst of Krishna's, Ward said, "Carey got no sleep again last night." Carey himself said of them, "Compared with Europeans, they are a larger sort of children. We are obliged to encourage, strengthen, counteract, disapprove, advise, teach, and yet all so as to retain their warm affection. We have much to exorcise our patience from the uncultivated state of their minds; but also much to rejoice us in respect to their conduct and their acquisition of evangelical knowledge. Even viewed at their worst, we can truly call them the excellent of Bengal."

While teaching at the college in Calcutta, Carey devoted his evenings to prayer and preaching, focusing much of his effort to bettering the condition of the Eurasians, especially those of Portuguese descent. The Eurasians were particularly unfortunate for they were disowned by their father's race and cast out by their mother's. No one would receive them, and they were in great need of comfort, companionship and help which a missionary could give them. Carey brought them human sympathy and understanding, and they listened gladly to his doctrine which was one of consolation for the outcast.

Among his many duties on his Serampore week-ends was the care of the sick. The blind, the lame, the halt came to him for help, and while he administered to their bodies he also gave them spiritual medicine for their souls. One of Carey's early interests was medical lore. While he was never trained as a doctor, still, under the tutelage of Dr. John Thomas, he learned a great deal to aid him in administering to the bodies of the Indians.

The mission workers, wishing to train native believers for Christian service, often took them along on itinerant tours — a helpful experience for the new Christians. These native believers were a valuable proof of the power of the Gospel, and a sample of the fruit of Christ's transforming power among the Indians. The fact that the villagers could hear the story of Christ from one of their own people greatly enhanced the value of the missionaries labors.

Carey had great hope for the future. He had visioned, when gazing at his homemade map on the wall above his cobbler's bench, a world brought under Christ's bounds. Now in his mind's eye he could see the Orient won for God. True, his converts had been few, and the result not at all glorious. Nevertheless, these were but tangible results and not worthy to be compared to the thousands of transformed lives throughout the Orient. He *knew* what the purifying stream of the Gospel could do for the people.

Little did Carey realize that he was already sowing the seeds that would germinate into oppression among the Indian rulers and the people themselves. Success and victory in the spread of the Gospel are always matched by the forces of evil in an attempt to destroy them.

In 1806 the trouble began. Lord Wellesley had retired in 1805. He had been a gracious friend and host of the missionaries, not in the least objecting to their work in the East India Company's territory, even though it was against the rules. He had even allowed open preaching in Calcutta. The Company had not approved his tolerance nor shared these ideas, however. They felt that Fort William College was an unnecessary expense.

With Lord Wellesley out of the way, their reaction at once set in. Passports were demanded from the missionaries

for the privilege of traveling in the Company's territories.
In some sections mission work was entirely prohibited. The
new Governor-General sided with the Company and said
that he would not authorize missionary establishments con-
trary to the privileges granted the Company by parliament.

The matter came to a head when a vessel under the command of Captain Wickes arrived with two new missionaries,
Chater and Robertson. The captain was refused clearance
and the missionaries were ordered to return. When the new
missionaries landed nevertheless, controversy over their
landing reached such a height that Carey was summoned on
August 26 and commanded to seek "that the Mission preach
no more to the native people, nor distribute pamphlets, nor
send out native preachers. The Governor-General does
not interfere with the prejudice of the natives, and he
must request Mr. Carey and his associates to abstain likewise from any interference with them."

In a highly dejected state Carey reached Serampore at
midnight with this distastrous news. When he aroused
his colleagues he laid the matter before them. This called
for a new forward-looking strategy. Carey and the other
missionaries resorted to prayer.

They asked, "Are we back where we were at the beginning, with a conflict on between us and the government
as represented by the officers of the East India Company?"
Fortunately the mission had been located in Danish territory, and the government there had promised them full
protection. Carey sent word to this effect to India's
governor, reminding him diplomatically that the Mission
was under the Danish king.

A compromise was finally effected. The government authorities admitted no complaint had been lodged against the
missionaries. Carey's group was permitted to advance their
work at Serampore. Likewise they continued to distribute
the Scriptures, preaching in their own precincts, and in

private rooms or houses in Calcutta. They could not, however, proclaim the Gospel openly in that city. Their
Indian converts could preach if they so desired on their
own initiative, the order stated, but they could no longer
be sent out by the mission with its special blessing.

This fell like a death knell upon the mission. Marshman
said, "In a moment we all became dead as respects
spreading the Gospel." All their plans for the growth of
the work throughout India were brought to a sudden and
abrupt halt. Carey wrote his homeland supporters, saying:

"We are all of us prisoners at Serampore, and you have
sent us two new brethren to keep us company. We are in
much the same situation as the Apostles when commanded
not to teach nor preach any more in the Name. The opening
doors for usefulness which a few days ago engaged our
attention and animated our exertions, are closed by this
cruel message."

He counseled calmness and moderation, adding:

"To act in open defiance of the Governor-General might
occasion a positive law against evangelizing the native
peoples, and at once break up the Mission which has been
settled at so great expense. On the other hand, if we yield
a little to the present storm, it may blow over, and we may
not only enjoy our present privileges, but obtain the liberty
we have so long wished for."

Then came soul-testing days when the flickering light of
the mission seemed almost to be extinguished. Here and
there tiny sparks appeared in spite of the darkness, however. Since further progress in India seemed barred, the
missionaries scanned fields beyond. They had thought of
Burma and possibly China as new realms for their labors.
So it was decided to send Missionary Chater to Burma "to
spy out the land." His orders were to examine the pos-
sibilites of the work there, with a view toward transferring

the group to that field. In due time Robertson returned to
the homeland.

As if to show God's leading in this move, on the very
day of Chater's sailing for Rangoon, a Burmese who understood Hindustani arrived at Serampore and offered to translate the Gospels, now in Bengali, into Burmese. Chinese
artisans also offered to teach the Bengali to cut wood blocks
for the Chinese Gospel.

This was the noble reward that came out of the dark oppression which the East India Company had thrown upon
the missionaries. The oppression was a blessing in the
disguise of persecution. God opened the way at the very
moment when it seemed all avenues for evangelizing the
Orient were to be blocked by government order.

In Bombay a new official, Sir James Mackentosh a recent arrival, espoused their cause. He invited Carey to bring
his mission to Bombay. This, of course, Carey could not
do, but he recommended one of the workers, a Doctor
Taylor, to represent the mission in Bombay. The doctor
soon became a warm friend of Mackentosh, taught him Sanskrit, sent for a press and Persian type, and kept the interest
growing in that city.

Some years before when Carey was using his Calcutta
evenings to preach in the city, he had directed his efforts
to Lall Bazaar, a disreputable section given over to saloons
and brothels, frequented by the sailors of all nations who
thronged the town, and by its own motley population as
well. So many crowded to hear Carey's preaching, including
Hindus and Mohammedans, that a bamboo building was
erected to house them.

"Multitudes used to hang upon the words that came from
our lips," said Carey when they suggested the erection of the
preaching shelter, "and would stand in the thickwedged
crowds for hours together in the heat."

Now, since open-air preaching was forbidden, the missionaries decided to build a Union Chapel in Lall Bazaar. It had been in their thoughts for some time, and occasionally gifts had been received for this purpose.

With these slight indications of victory a new storm was brewing. Shortly a new Governor-General, Lord Minto, arrived. Those opposed to the mission work seized upon his unfamiliarity with the situation to excite his fears. They laid particular stress on the insidious work of the press at Serampore.

"The public peace will be threatened," they told him, "particularly among the Mussulmans, till its publications are suppressed."

In proof of their claim they showed him a pamphlet in which a Mohammedan was depicted as an imposter and tyrant. "To let such matters be disseminated is simply to invite trouble," the enemies of the Mission told Lord Minto.

The government at this time was especially sensitive to the native feeling and when tides of irritation swept the nation the officials were immediately active in uncovering the source. A mutiny which had been caused by an infringement of a seemingly insignificant Hindu custom had just been quelled near Madras. All English officials were being especially careful at this time not to offend the natives. Carey was summoned. He had never even heard of the pamphlet, but upon investigation found that the offending language had been inserted without the Mission's knowledge. The tract was destroyed and due apologies were made. Nevertheless, on September 11, 1807, the press at Serampore was ordered brought to Calcutta, and all preaching services and efforts for conversion in Serampore were commanded to cease.

Imagine the dejection that greeted this latest announcement!

"We are a few poor fish disposed to everyone," Marshman wrote friends. Ward said, "Carey wept like a child after he heard the sad news, knowing, as Marshman put it, 'that the press removed to Calcutta would not be safe a day.' As long as it remained at Serampore many obstacles had to be surmounted before it could be touched, but in Calcutta it would only be for someone to fancy something offensive in a publication and get the ear of a government officer and the press might be seized and its printers deported."

After prayer and thoughtful discussion, the group decided to prepare a paper telling of their work, and to send a representative to Lord Minto in person. Before this could be done the situation in Calcutta grew worse. Rumors spread that the missionaries were to be expelled from India. The soldiers at Ft. William entered into the dispute with cries of "Ten pounds for catching the Methodists!" "Bravo, boys, watch for them," and such rabble-rousing slogans.

"Had some Rajah or Nadov forbidden our teaching," wrote gentle Hannah Marshman, "we should not have wondered. But that those who should be our nursing fathers should do this is most strange."

These were sad days indeed for the anxious little band at Serampore. Through the darkness Carey and his compatriots recognized that only God could bring the light of victory. Carey said of these difficult times:

"Many would rejoice to see us expelled. We have no security but in God. The experience of Abram who was alone when called, supports me. I have for many months had my mind drawn to Isaiah 40:28, 'He fainteth not, neither is weary.' I have no doubt but that our troubles will tend to the furtherance of the Gospel; but to what extent they may be carried it is impossible to say. We mean to inform Lord Minto that we are prepared to suffer in this cause rather than abandon our work; but we hope to do all in the most respectful manner possible. Such a letter was never written by a Christian government before. Roman

Catholics have persecuted other Christians as heretics; but since the days of heathen Rome, no Christian government, however corrupt, has, so far as I know, prohibited the attempts to spread Christianity among the heathen. We are all in mourning. I do not know that anything ever so affected me. My mind is full of tumultuous cogitations. I trust Jehovah will appear to us."

The missionary's trust in Jehovah was not misplaced. He and Marshman were granted an interview with Lord Minto, who, after listening to them, was convinced he was misinformed. He discussed the matter with his council whose decision was favorable with the missionaries. The council requested only that a copy of all publications be submitted to them. On October 14, 1817, Carey wrote to his faithful friend, Andrew Fuller, of this victory:

"I rejoice to inform you that the storm is gone over. The Governor of Serampore has received a letter from our Government revoking their order concerning our press, and only requiring to be apprised of what we print . . . We had little expectation of this formal revocation, though we hoped it might not be enforced. I believe the obstacles which yet remain will gradually be removed. There are, however, many in the country who would rejoice to see Christianity wholly expelled. But our confidence is in God. I preached this evening from Isaiah, 'Is My Hand shortened, etc.' "

Repercussions in England were seemingly much more important than those in India. Friends and opponents of the mission fought for and against it. Many were the arguments presented by those who believed in the Mission.

"Carey and his son have been in Bengal fourteen years," wrote Southey, one of Carey's supporters, "the others only nine. They have all had a difficult language to acquire, before they could speak to the people; to preach and argue therein required a thorough and familiar knowledge. The wonder is not that they have done so little, but so much. The anti-missionaries cull from their journals and letters all that is ridiculous, sectarian and trifling; call them fools, madmen, tinkers and schismatics; and keep out of sight their love of man and zeal for God, their self-devotement, their indefatigable industry and unequalled learning.

"These 'low-born and low-bred mechanics' have translated the whole Bible into Bengali, and by this time have printed it. They are printing the New Testament in Sanskrit, Oriya, Marathi, Hindi and Gujarati; and are translating it into Persic, Telugu, Kanarese, Chinese and the tongue of the Sikhs and of the Burmans; and in four of these languages they are going on with the whole Bible.

"Extraordinary as this is, it will appear more so when it is remembered that of these men, one was originally a shoemaker, another a printer, and the third, the master of a charity school. Only fourteen years have elapsed since Thomas and Carey set foot in India, and in that time these missionaries have acquired this gift of tongues; in fourteen years these 'low-born, low-bred mechanics' have done more toward spreading the knowledge of the Scriptures among the heathen than has been accomplished, or even attempted, by all the world's princes and potentates, and all its universities and establishments into the bargain."

Chapter 7

THE GOSPEL BY THE PRINTED PAGE

AT HEART William Carey was a Bible translator. This was his first and supreme love. As a child he had mastered a Latin vocabulary produced by Dyche, and as an apprentice lad he had carefully traced the characters of the Greek alphabet that he might carry them to the home of a learned and scholarly friend, who was to explain them. When he arrived in India he set himself at the task of mastering the dialects and languages of that nation and surrounding nations.

It was not long until Carey's brilliant mentality had placed him in the first ranks of Oriental linguists; until William Carey's great ability attained its full stature. While he must carry on the ordinary duties of his teaching, and likewise undergo the humiliation of criticism in the homeland, he spent his happiest hours in giving the Word of God to the people with whom he labored.

Carey had cause for great sorrow during the tumultuous days of this period. On December 7, 1807, his wife died. While this might have seemed like release from a burden, still it grieved him. He had loved Dorothy for many years. He had cared for and protected her as a father would a child, for her mind had been affected during most of the time they had been in India. Friends had wanted Carey to put her in an institution, but he could never bring himself to do this, for she was his wife, the mother of his children.

To the end Carey treated her with the greatest love and respect. In writing to Andrew Fuller, Carey said:

"She had been in a state most depressing for the last twelve years. Indeed the turn of her mind was such as prevented her from feeling even those ideal pleasures which sometimes attend maniacal persons."

He wrote to his son Felix, who was then in Burma, "During the last illness she was almost always asleep. I suppose, during the fourteen days she lay in a severe fever, she was not more than twenty-four hours awake."

Through the many years her mind was befogged Carey was the most tender and compassionate. Marshman said of the situation:

"It will serve to give something of the strength and energy of Dr. Carey's character that the arduous Biblical and literary labors in which he had been engaged since his arrival in Serampore were executed while an insane wife, frequently wrought up to the state of most depressing excitement, was in a room near his study."

The sadness of those days was if anything greater because of Felix's absence. Though Carey rejoiced at the noble work Felix was then doing, still his father-heart longed for the young son. Felix had gone to Burma with Chater, who had returned from his scouting expedition with enthusiastic reports of missionary work there.

In fact, during the governmental difficulties the workers had seriously considered moving the entire mission there. When Chater went back to Burma he begged for a colleague. The enterprise appealed to Felix, for "he longed to be out somewhere." And with his love of adventure, his linguistic ability and the medical training which he had taken, he was pre-eminently fitted for the task. So, though Carey needed his son in the printing plant, he agreed to allow Felix to go to Burma. Carey's farewell sermon to his son was on the text, "Take heed to thyself and to thy doctrine." His written injunctions to the young man were as full of wise counsel for today as then. Carey said:

"Let the Burmese language occupy your most precious time and your most arduous solicitude . . . Do not be content with its most superficial acquiring. Make it yours, root and branch. Listen with prying curiosity to the forms of speech, the construction and accent of the people . . . And unless you frequently use what you acquire, it will profit you little.

"Observe a rigid economy. Missionary funds are the most sacred on earth. Cultivate brotherly love. Preach the neverfailing word of the Cross. Be instant in season and out. Do not despise the patient instruction of one Burman. Make memoranda of all you see. Be meek and gentle among the people. Cultivate the utmost cordiality with them as your equals. Never let European pride and superiority appear at the Mission House, Rangoon."

As the months rolled by Carey's loneliness was dispelled. In the year that the Serampore Mission had been started, Lady Charlotte Rumohr, of a noble family of Denmark, had come to the settlement. Lady Charlotte's mother was a countess, and her sister was wife of the chamberlain of the king of Denmark. As a child Charlotte had been delicate, and from the night she was injured when her father's home was destroyed by fire, Charlotte had been an invalid unable to walk up and down stairs.

She had sought help in various places, and was finally advised to go to India. Governor Bie of Serampore, a kinsman, took it upon himself to welcome her to the settlement. Lady Charlotte built a fine home on the Hoogly River close to the Mission, and at Governor Bie's suggestion took English lessons from Carey. From him also she learned a new and better understanding of the Christian religion. Likewise she took a zealous interest in the work. Being thoroughly converted, she was baptized in June, 1801, and was the first European woman in India to receive this gracious rite at the hand of the missionary Carey. Thereafter she was an enthusiastic friend of the mission. She learned Bengali that she might be more helpful.

In his loneliness after his wife's death, Carey cast his eyes toward this faithful assistant who had helped carry many of the burdens of the Mission. Shortly thereafter the announcement of his and Lady Charlotte's engagement brought a storm of consternation among Carey's friends. They even went so far as to send a round-robin letter of protest. Gentle Hannah Marshman signed it, though she questioned the wisdom of the letter. She wrote in her diary, saying:

"How did my whole body tremble when I was called upon to sign the letter." The following Sunday she added, "My husband preached but I could not listen. I was in such an agitation about Dr. Carey."

These entries give a glimpse of the turmoil into which the little colony was thrown by the news of the forthcoming marriage. They did not object to Lady Rumohr, for she had been their good friend and had been one of them for many years. But they felt that her invalidism would be a handicap to Dr. Carey's work. Once again his wife might become a burden. Then too, some of the criticism was because of his wife's recent death. Carey talked the matter over with his associates, however, and the protest was withdrawn.

He and Lady Charlotte were married in May, 1808. His wife became a great help and comfort to him. She immediately gave her home to the Mission, the rent from the spacious house going to support native preachers. She also sent money to buy a business for Carey's brother, Thomas, in England, whose government pension as a disabled soldier was not sufficient for his needs.

She took it upon herself to support a school at Serampore

and one at Cutwa for the education of Hindu girls. Perhaps her greatest assistance was her help in the work of translation. She was an excellent linguist and knew Danish, Italian and French well. Her knowledge of the Scriptures in these languages made her of great value to her scholarly husband.

She was hopelessly fragile, often being compelled to keep to her couch for months at a time. Her spirit was courageous and cheerful, however, her mind active and keen. Daily, morning and evening when she was able, she was out in a carriage along the river bank, often on her way to the schools or homes of the natives. God gave Carey this fine companionship for the next thirteen years.

God indeed was in this marriage, for Lady Charlotte rendered Carey valuable assistance by lifting from his shoulders many burdens in the study of the original Bible text. During the pleasant years that they were together she was a constant source of sympathy and interested help.

Carey's children, now grown men, were at this time a great source of satisfaction. Felix was prospering in Burma, and his father joyfully wrote friends of the young man's activities. Young William was ordained, and in 1807 was married and went as a missionary worker and business helper to one of Carey's first converts in the neighborhood of his own early labors as an indigo planter. Carey said to him:

"You are in a task, my son, very dear to my remembrance, because my first Indian years were spent in its neighborhood. Be steady in your work and leave the results to God." The place in which William was stationed was lonely, however, and terrorized by buffalo and brigands. Later he wrote his father asking for a safer place, but Carey replied sternly:

"You and Mary will be a thousand times safer committing yourselves to God in the path of duty than neglecting duty to take care of yourselves."

Dr. Carey himself had gone through the trials and difficulties and he knew that the safest place for a Christian was in the center of God's will. He told William of his own trials in the same neighborhood, ending with the ringing advice, "Mount your horse and be out on God's work."

Carey was honored during these years by having a Doctor of Divinity degree conferred on him by Brown University. He received this honor both because of his fame for mission work and for his translations which had spread so far.

At this time William Carey, the lad who had come up through great hardness from the cobbler's bench, was one of the most renowned men of his generation. Among Christian circles he was spoken of as the man of the hour. God had prospered him and spread his fame throughout Christendom. The stream of Carey's active life was halted on June 26, 1809, however, when he was seized with a fever, and for two weeks lay so desperately ill that it was thought he would not recover. He had just finished the second edition of the Bengali Bible on which he had been laboring unceasingly in the humid heat of the season. When his colleagues asked him that evening what his further plans were he replied that he had enough translation work planned for twenty years, but his exhausting toil had done its work. In a few hours he was delirious. His hallucinations during the fever were rather odd. He wrote of them afterwards, saying:

"In my delirium, I was busily employed, as I perfectly remember, in carrying a communication from God to all the princes and governments in the world, requiring them instantly to abolish every political establishment of religion, and to sell the parish and other churches to the first body of Christians who would purchase them. Also, to declare war infamous, and military officers the destroyers of the race . . . a few princes in Germany were refractory, but my attendants struck them dead."

After his recovery, he always maintained that these brain storms were not mere delusions. "They were truths," he insisted, "whose force I wish to feel and for whose triumph I must strive to the end of my life."

Of Carey's illness, Ward wrote Fuller at length, concluding:

"When we thought we had lost Carey, we were ready to ask, 'Who will finish his Marathi and Bengal dictionaries? Who will complete his Sanskrit and Oriya Old Testament? Who will carry on the Hindi, Marathi and all the other translations?'"

It seems almost impossible to conceive of one individual carrying on such an extensive program of linguistic activities as engaged Carey's mind. He not only mastered the Oriental languages of the section in which he was working, but he took time to organize the grammar of these languages for publication. In all of his work of translation Carey felt that he owed a heavy debt of gratitude to his "Serampore brethren," as he called his colleagues. In most of his translations various members of the missionary staff at Serampore worked by his side. For instance, during this time he says that he engaged a Mr. Gilchrist in the translation of the Scriptures into the Hindustani language. Later another assisted in translating the Bible into the Persian. Carey affirms:

"We accordingly hired two Moonshees to assist us in it, and each of us took our share. Brother Marshman took Matthew and Luke; Brother Ward, Mark; I took the remaining part of the New Testament into the Hindustani. I undertook no part of the Persian, but instead thereof engaged in translating it into the Marathi language, the per-

son who assisted me being a Marathian. Brother Marshman
has finished Matthew, and instead of Luke has begun the
Acts. Brother Ward has done part of John, and I have
done the Epistles, and about six chapters of the Revelation,
and have proceeded as far as the Second Epistle of Cor-
inthians in the revisal. They have done a few chapters in
the Persian and I a few into Marathi."

While Carey in his own humility and large-heartedness
was ever ready to acknowledge the co-operation of his
colleagues, there could be no question that the introduction
of the Scriptures to the people of India was mainly due to
his own labors. Many times friends in England raised
objections to his employing the natives who were not
Christians in the work of translating. Yet Carey always
answered these criticisms as follows:

"Whatever help we employ I have never yet suffered a
single word or a single mode of construction without having
examined it and seeing through it. I read every proof
sheet twice or thrice myself, and correct every letter with
my own hand. Brother Marshman or myself compare with
the Greek or Hebrew, and Brother Ward reads every
sheet. Three of the translations, mainly the Bengali,
Hindustani and the Sanskrit, I translate with my own hands,
the two last immediately from the Greek and the Hebrew
Bible is before me while I translate the Bengali."

In 1811, being fully alert to the importance of laying a
firm foundation for future Bible translations in the Orient,
Dr. Carey resolved to prepare a grammar of all of the
different languages in which the Scriptures had been or
might be translated.

"With little success," he wrote to Dr. Ryland, "those who
follow us will have to wade through the same labor that
I have in order to stand merely upon the same ground that
I now stand upon. If, however, elementary books are

provided the labor will be greatly contracted and a person will be able in a short time to acquire that which has cost me years of study and toil. The necessity which lies upon me of acquiring so many languages obliges me to study and write the grammar of each of them, and to attend closely to the irregularity and peculiarities.

"I have therefore already published grammars of three of them, namely the Sanskrit, Bengali and the Marathi. To these I have resolved to add grammars of Telinga, Kurmata, Orissa, Punjabee, Kashneera, Gujeratee, Nepalese and Assam languages. Two of these are now in the press and I hope to have two or three more of them out by the end of next year. This may not only be useful in the way I have stated but may serve to furnish an answer to the question that has been more than once repeated, 'How can these men translate into so great a number of languages?'"

In the same letter Carey went on to outline his future plans. He said that he was at that time printing a dictionary of the Bengali, which would be a large and heavy book. He added that in order to secure a gradual perfection to the translations, he had long been collecting materials for a universal dictionary of the Oriental languages which were derived from the Sanskrit.

"I mean to take the Sanskrit, of course," he wrote concerning this work, "as the ground work, and to give the different acceptations of every word with examples of their applications . . . and then to give the synonyms in the different languages derived from the Sanskrit with the Hebrew and Greek terms answering them too, always putting the word derived from the Sanskrit first, and then those derived from other sources. I intend always to give the etymology of the Sanskrit term, so that of the term deduced from it in the Gothic languages, will be evident."

He went on to say that whether he should live to carry out this tremendous task was doubtful, but that he aimed

to begin it and so arrange his research material that who-
ever came after him could finish the task. He continued,
"Should I live to accomplish this and the translations at
hand I think I can then say, 'Lord, now lettest thy servant
depart in peace.'"

It was the custom of the Serampore Mission to publish
what they called or designated Memoirs so that friends
might have a true idea of the prodigious labors that were
being carried on at the Mission. In the seventh Memoir the
astounding erudition and output centering in William
Carey's translating is shown.

The Memoir indicated that the fifth edition of the New
Testament in the Bengali, consisting of 5,000 copies printed
some years before, had already been exhausted; that the
second edition of the different parts of the Old Testament
had been unavailable for some time. It affirmed that a new
edition of the entire Bengali Scripture was necessary. This
would be the sixth edition of the New Testament, the third
of the Psalms, and some of the other parts of the Old Testament, and would consist of from four to six thousand copies.
It would comprise a book of some 1,300 pages.

In the Sanskrit, the last two volumes of the Old Testament had been printed, the Memoir pointed out, and the
first edition of the New Testament was already exhausted,
which would entail the printing of 2,000 new copies.
Similarly, in the Hindustani language the New Testament
had been published two years before and all of the copies
were exhausted, which would call for a printing of the New
Testament. In the Orissa language, the whole of the Scriptures had long been published. The first edition of the New
Testament was exhausted, and a new edition of 4,000 copies
of this was now on the press. Likewise the last volume of
the Old Testament in the Marathi language was published

many months ago, so that a new version of the whole Scripture in that language was now completed.

"In these five languages the whole of the Scriptures are now published and in circulation. In the last four of them second editions of the New Testament are in the press, and in the first Bengali begun 26 years ago the sixth edition of the New Testament."

Then the Memoir went on to show the progress in ten other languages. The first was the Chinese, in which a translation of the Old Testament had been completed several years before. In the Sikh, the New Testament had already been published, and parts of the Old Testament were in the process of publication. In the Pushtoo, or Afghan language, the New Testament was already published and parts of the Old Testament were in the process of publication. Similarly in the Kunkuna, in the Wuch, in the Assam, in the Bikaneer, as well as in the language of Nepal of the Harotte, of the Marwar, of the Kashmeer and of the Oojein folk, the Bible in whole or in part was either already published or in the process of being printed.

Many other languages were at the moment engaging the attention of Carey.

That the reader might have at least a casual sight of the prodigious output of Carey and his associates as he directed their activities, I give the following quotation from this report:

"The Jumboo, Kanoj, and Khassee, printed as far as John; the Khosol, Bhutuneer, Dogura and Majudha to Mark, and the Kumaoon, Judwal, and Munippra to Matthew.

"In these ten versions, therefore, a sufficient progress is made to render the completion of them is nowise difficult. In comparing this Memoir with the last it will be seen that in several of the languages therein the translation has been discontinued. To this the brethren had been constrained by the low state of translation funds arising principally from the heavy expenses occasioned by the new edition of the Sanskrit the Bengali and the Hindu, and the Orissa languages now in the press. In discontinuing these, however, they had been guided by the due consideration of the importance and distinctiveness of the different languages in which they were engaged, as well as the ease with which a Pundit could be procured, should the public enable them to resume again."

Besides these versions fonts of types for other languages had been prepared at the Mission Press — in the Cingalese and the Persian, for instance, for Henry Martyn's version in that language.

Leaping ahead over several years, after the publication of this Memoir, we see that the work of the press continued unremitting, until at the time of Carey's death the entire Scriptures or parts of them had been translated into forty languages or dialects, and between the editions of the ninth and Tenth Memoirs, an interval of nine years, no less than 99,000 volumes, or more than 31,000,000 pages of the Old and New Testaments passed through the presses.

In the Society's annual report for 1825 a letter from Carey is quoted in which he states "The New Testament will soon be printed in thirty-four languages, and the Old Testament in eight, besides versions in three varieties of the Hindustani New Testament."

In the long view this steady progress was heartening, but as the individual days, weeks, and even years passed, misfortunes heavy and untoward, befell the Mission. One of the greatest occurred March 11, 1812.

A fire raced through the printing works, burning for three days, leaving only a shell of blackened walls and a few documents. For hours the workers labored to quench the flames. They did prevent the fire from spreading to the Mission house and the school dormitories. Some of the presses were saved, title deeds to the property and a few ledgers, but almost everything else was consumed.

A stock of paper just received from England went up in the blaze, as also did new type in Tamil and Chinese. Fonts of Hebrew, Greek, Persian, Arabic, Nagari, Telegu and other vernaculars were burned. Similarly, valuable manuscripts containing parts of the Old and New Testaments in the Indian languages and in the Sanskrit, pages of various dictionaries and grammars, and all of Dr. Carey's dictionary of the Sanskrit and its Indian cognate were consumed.

The destruction to these valuable manuscripts was probably the greatest loss of all. They represented years of labor, and required many years to replace. Carey, busy with his college duties in Calcutta, knew nothing of the calamity until Marshman arrived the next morning with the appalling news. The doctor was overwhelmed. In writing of the catastrophe to friends in England, he said:

"Our printing office was totally destroyed by fire, and all its property amounting to at least Rs. 60,000 to 70,000. This is a heavy blow, as it will stop our printing the Scriptures for a long time. Twelve months' hard labor will not reinstate us, not to mention loss of property, Mss. etc., which we shall scarcely ever surmount. I wish to be still and know that the Lord He is God, and to bow to His will in everything. He will no doubt bring good out of this evil and make it promote His interests, but at present the providence is exceedingly dark."

Dr. Carey secured leave-of-absence from his college duties, and heartened by the word of a colleague, "However vexing it may be, the road a second time traveled is usually taken with more confidence and ease than at first," started on the task of repair. Calcutta was searched for printable materials, and a letter was dispatched to England for help. Carey and Marshman hurried to Serampore, and much to the astonishment of the passive and fatalistic natives the work of rehabilitation was immediately taken up and pressed with astonishing vigor.

Friends sprang to the Mission's aid. Letters, money, printing material, furniture and all other requisites flowed in. Within a few months they were printing again in the vernaculars. By the end of the year their type in all of the Oriental languages was completed. The work of Carey's Indian colleagues in the re-translation was such a great improvement over the first that Dr. Carey was saved much labor in revision.

The most gracious boon of all was the effect of the news in England. The churches generally, without regard to denominational lines and beliefs, sprang to the Mission's relief. In two months the goal of $50,000.00 was attained. Andrew Fuller announced to the Committee, his eyes sparkling, his face beaming:

"Brethren, the money is all raised, and so constantly are contributions still pouring in that we must in honesty publish an intimation that the need is removed."

The benefit was greater along other lines, however, than in the immediate financial aid received for rebuilding the printing establishment. It was in the dramatic awakening of England to what the Mission had accomplished and that in which it was immediately engaged. In the blaze of the fire the greatness of the project undertaken by Carey and his colleagues burst with brilliant luster.

"This fire has given your undertaking a celebrity which nothing else could," Andrew Fuller wrote to Dr. Carey.

But with the good news of the people's heartfelt interest and support Fuller later sent a warning, saying:

"When the people ascribed 'ten thousands to David.'

he admonished, 'it wrought envy in Saul,' and proved a source of long and sore affliction. If some new trials were to follow, I should not be surprised, but if we keep humble and near to God, we have nothing to fear."

Andrew Fuller's apprehensions were verified. Although the Governor-General had rescinded his strict orders in regard to the press and preaching, and despite the heart-felt support to the Mission, aroused by the fire, enemies in England were still at work. Believing that the opposition had died down, new missionaries volunteered. Upon arrival they were immediately ordered returned by the officials of the East India Company and the English government. One of these in particular, W. Johns, blamed the Mission for being shipped back, contending that if sufficient pressure had been brought to bear upon the government officials he could have remained in India. He especially censured Marshman who had been in charge of the affair, and spread a report about him in England that so worried Dr. Carey as to make him alarmingly ill.

A gleam of joy burst upon this gloom, however. Carey's son, Jabez, though an exemplary youth, had shown a particular zeal for missionary work. At his own request he had taken up the study of law in Calcutta, where he had made a notable success, but a change of heart came in 1812. The following year he felt that God would have him volunteer as a missionary to the Molucca Islands. Carey said:

"The lad's conduct for a year and a half has left no doubt of his Christian spirit."

His father wished to be sure that his son fully understood what he was doing, however. He talked to him seriously of the privations and trials of a new field, and also laid before him what he was giving up in a material way, for the lad's legal prospects were bright, since a judge of the Supreme Court had become greatly interested in him.

Jabez remained firm in his decision. He was ordained shortly thereafter and married, and he and his wife sailed to the new field. Dr. Carey was greatly elated to think that another of his sons had followed him in the missionary course. He told his son that he would rather have Jabez be a missionary than Chief Justice of Bengal. Though still far from well, Dr. Carey wrote Jabez, January 24, 1814, a long letter in regard to the conduct of his new duties:

"You are engaged in a most important undertaking in which you will have not only my prayers for your success, but those of all who love our Lord Jesus and who know of your engagement.

"Trust always in Christ. Be pure of heart. Live a life of prayer and of devotedness to God. Be gentle and un-assuming, yet firm and manly.

"You are now married. Be not content to bear yourself toward your wife with propriety, but let love be the spring of all your conduct . . . The first impressions of love arising from character will endure and increase.

"Behave affably to all, cringingly and unsteadily to none . . . A gentleman is the next best character after a Christian, and the latter includes the former. Money never makes a gentleman, much less does a fine appearance, but an en-larged understanding joined to engaging manners.

"Shun all indolence and love of ease, and never try to act the part of the great and gay in the world.

"Your great work is that of a Christian minister. God has conferred on you a great favor in committing to you this ministry. Take heed to fulfill it."

Carey had been through the fires of persecution him-self and he spoke from experience of the undergirding grace of Jesus Christ. Now that he was advancing in age he could remain happy in the firm knowledge that God had given him sons who would help carry on the work that he had begun. There were yet, however, twenty years of Christian service that God was to give to this famous yet humble missionary.

Many tasks were at hand, many untried avenues of activity remained. But God had been his undergirding, his support and his firm foundation. Now William could face the sunset of life firm in the knowledge that Jesus Christ who had said, "Forward into India," would give him strength to finish that which he had undertaken in the name of God.

Chapter 8

TRAINING NATIVE WORKERS

THE GENIUS of William Carey is to be found in the
fact that he multiplied himself through the efforts of others.
Early in his career he discovered that if he would give
the Bible to the numerous people of the Orient, he could
better do so through associating with himself others who were
qualified to handle these various languages. In the course
of time Dr. Carey's program broadened to take in the
younger Christians. In fact, he recognized that it would
be wiser to mold youth than to try radically to reform age.

Consequently, in May, 1811, he wrote to Dr. Ryland,
saying: "A year ago we opened a free school in Calcutta.
This year we added to it a school for girls. There are now
in it about a hundred and forty boys and near thirty girls.
One of our deacons, Mr. Leonard, a most valuable and
active man, superintends the boys, and a very pious woman,
a member of our church, is over the girls."

Similarly, Carey discovered that there were a number of
people who were outcasts, completely down trodden. Many
of these were Eurasians. They were the children of Europeans who had married natives of the various nations.
Carey's plan of education took them in. During the next
few years many similar schools were sponsored by the
Mission. In 1817 there were forty-five such institutions
established in the district about Calcutta which number
was thereafter greatly increased.

The spread of this educational movement took on broad proportions, until a school followed the opening of every preaching station. By this means Carey trained the natives in the Christian way. He found that he could lead them to make decisions for Christ far better after having taught them in the schools than he could by the mere process of preaching against the stone wall of native indifference.

In 1818 the press at Serampore issued the first vernacular newspaper. This was called the *News Mirror,* which was shortly changed to the *Friend of India.* Marshman was entrusted with the editorship. Henceforth the *Friend of India* sponsored the work of the Mission and became a rich ally in propagating the Gospel.

For some time now Dr. Carey and his associates had felt the growing need of an advanced training center for the native converts. Through the years various schools had been operating on a lower-grade level. Several churches had been formed and the number of converts multiplied. By 1817 Carey felt the acute need of an institution in which native Christians who desired to devote themselves to evangelistic and pastoral work, and those having gifts and graces for such, might be suitably trained. In that year Carey wrote to Dr. Ryland, saying:

"We have bought a piece of ground adjoining the Mission premises on which there is an old house, and which for the present may be sufficient for the instruction of those whom God may give unto us. But we should be glad to see before our removal by death a better house erected. I can see that the work of duly preparing a large body — as large a body as possible — of Christian natives of India for Christian pastors and itinerants is of immense proportions. The English missionaries will never be able to instruct the whole of India."

He went on to say that the resources and the numbers of missionaries required for the instruction of the millions of

India could never be supplied from England, and that India would never be turned from her gross idolatry to serve the true and living God, "unless the grace of God rest abundantly upon converted natives to qualify them for mission work, and unless by the instrumentality of those who care for India they be sent forth to the field. In my judgment therefore it is on native evangelists that the weight of the great work must ultimately rest."

With this letter Dr. Carey informed the home Society that he and his associates were founding a college at Serampore. During the following year a prospectus of the school was issued, setting forth the training courses contemplated. It was proposed to instruct students in the doctrines they were to combat, and the dogmas they were to teach. Great stress was laid upon the desirability of acquiring a knowledge of Sanskrit, for without this knowledge those dealing with natives would be placed at a great disadvantage.

Similarly, Carey believed that if the Gospel were to prevail in India, it would be only in the way of demonstrating the excellence of the Christian religion above all other systems.

The instruction was to be in the vernacular, and courses were to be given in vernacular dialects, as well as the sacred classic language. Nor was instruction in English to be neglected.

The institution was to be established purely on a nonsectarian foundation, with the right of conscience being most carefully respected. After a detailed calculation was made of the annual expense, Carey appealed to the public for support. At the same time the doctor and his colleagues gave $12,500.00 from their personal resources for the work. In addition, Carey asked the government to assist in carrying the expense of the institution. The Danish governor, Colonel Kresting, was most cordial and consented to be the first governor of the college. The King of Denmark as well as the Royal College of Commerce at Copenhagen approved of this move.

Thus encouraged, Carey purchased a plot of land in the most eligible situation and laid plans for the college buildings. Marshman described the buildings thus:

"The center building intended for the public rooms was 130 feet in length and 120 in depth, the hall on the ground floor supported on arches and terminated on the south by a bow was 95 feet in length, 66 in breadth and 20 in height. It was originally intended for the library but is now occupied by classes. The hall above of the same dimensions and 26 feet in height was supported by two rows of Ionic columns. It was intended for the annual examinations."

He goes on to describe how the various-sized rooms were used not only for classrooms, but for assemblage places where the students might feel free to converse at will.

"The spacious grounds," Marshman continues, "were surrounded with iron railings and the front entrance was adorned with a noble gate which was cast at Birmingham. The scale upon which it was proposed to establish the college, and to which the size of the building was necessarily accommodated, corresponded with the breadth of all of the other enterprises of the Serampore missionaries — the Mission, the translations and the schools."

Carey had already been experimenting in training workers. He had sent out as many native converts as could be in any way useful until there were fifty natives employed in evangelization. These in the main were supported by the missionaries themselves.

An appeal was made to Christian friends everywhere to finance this new venture. In the appeal the following was stated:

"Dr. Carey and his brethren have begun a Christian

Seminary in Serampore and have placed it under their own inspection for giving Scriptural knowledge and correct doctrinal views to these native missionaries, that they may go out into the work prepared like Apollos, by Acquila and Priscilla, and 'taught the way of the Lord more perfectly.'

"It is not intended to give, except in rare instances, a learned education to these persons, but to give them that knowledge of the divine Word and the foundation principles of the system of redemption which is absolutely necessary to a Christian teacher, and without which the hope of the real good from him is small indeed."

In 1821 the King of Denmark gave a large house in the Serampore settlement to the missionaries for the college. Five years later he granted a charter of incorporation by which the permanency of the school was secured. Thus the college was placed upon the same basis as colleges and universities in Europe, and among other privileges it was given the right to confer degrees.

Before completion the cost of the buildings reached $100,000.00 of which the Serampore brethren contributed no less than $75,000. Dr. Carey served as president of the institution, as well as professor of divinity, and lecturer on botany, zoology and other sciences. Throughout the remainder of his life the institution was one of the prize services which the Mission rendered to the world.

During these years vexing problems arose. With the revision of the East India Company charter which resulted in the lifting of restrictions against missionary work, a number of helpers arrived at Serampore. Among them was a nephew of Dr. Carey named Yaltes, who like his uncle was from the shoemaker's bench. Randall, an engineer, arrived to take charge of the paper mill. Similarly a printer named Pearce, who was the son of Carey's good friend, Samuel Pearce, came to assist in the printing. Likewise a well-trained schoolteacher was sent from England who could fit himself into the educational program of the Mission.

These workers were most welcome. Carey himself was busier than ever with his college duties in Calcutta, at Serampore, and the many translations under his supervision. He was in constant supervision of twenty-two Scriptural translations including almost every Indian language, as well as the Chinese, and the native tongue of Afghanistan.

Though these newcomers fitted helpfully into the actual physical work, they did introduce a note of friction and discord into the peaceful community life. Johns, who had been earlier returned to England before the restrictions against missionaries were removed, resentfully spread reports against Carey and Ward, but especially toward Marshman. Some of the newcomers were in this way prejudiced against Carey before they arrived; some did not like community living.

Eventually four of them joined forces, separated themselves from the others and started a church in Calcutta. They established schools as rivals to Marshman's against whom they were especially prejudiced. They even operated a printing press. In no way unfavorably disposed toward Dr. Carey, these men even asked him to join them. But to outsiders it looked like a break in the mission life and greatly perturbed the doctor. Consequently Carey wrote to Dr. Ryland:

"I do not recollect in my whole life anything which has given me so much distress as this schism. Many sleepless nights have I spent in examining what we have done to give it occasion, but can discover nothing. The mission, however, is rent in twain, and exhibits the scandalous appearance of a body divided against itself. We could easily vindicate ourselves, but the vindication would be ours and their disgrace. We have therefore resolved to say nothing, but to leave the matter in God's hands."

Troubles of even a more heartbreaking nature fell upon

Carey. Rumors began to spread in England that the missionaries were making private fortunes, also that Carey was providing for the future of his sons, both financially as well as affording "soft positions for them." The exact opposite was the truth, for the missionaries, after supplying their own simple necessities, freely returned all earnings to the misson. Carey's earnings from his salary might have been considerable, especially after his appointment to the college in Calcutta. However, he wrote to his friends in England:

"I have devoted my all to the cause and so have my colleagues. I am now in my old age, destitute of a rupee. Were I to die today I should not have property enough for the purchase of a coffin. We are coarsely clad and certainly underfed."

Unfortunately, two of the Mission's staunchest friends in England, Sutcliff and Andrew Fuller, had passed away, so that Carey did not have them "to hold the ropes" as they had earlier agreed, while he was at the "bottom of the well." Indeed he was in the depths of the well at that moment. In fact, so greatly did all these discords prey upon his mind that he became seriously ill. At one time friends despaired of his life, but gradually the healing hand of God was laid upon his body.

His troubles, however, were not over. News from Felix was causing him some slight anxiety, though his work in Burma had been successful and he had found favor with the King. Through an accident his wife and children were drowned. Felix's mind was affected for several years, but eventually he returned to Serampore, to the joy of all the missionaries.

Troubles in England were by no means allayed. From the inception of the missionary project, Fuller, Sutcliff and Dr. Ryland had been practically the Committee in charge, but now with Sutcliff and Fuller deceased and the work grown to great dimensions, the Committee was increased to thirty-five, with a Finance Committee being added. Instead of the old friendly intimacy and ready helpfulness, the management was formal and businesslike. The Finance Committee demanded the precise terms of trust of the Indian property and advised that eight British trustees be appointed to serve with the three at Serampore. This was perhaps only business formality, but to the three leaders at Serampore, whose child the Mission and its work was, it was trying. Even Ryland, the last of the old guard in England, wrote forebodingly:

"I have unbounding fears for the future. I tremble for the Ark of God when it shall fall into the hands of mere counting-house men."

Further indications of the change in the home viewpoint was the "assigning" of Pearce and his wife when they arrived in August, 1817, to "reside in the Serampore family, Ward's colleagues in the press." This was an innovation that touched the Serampore family rather unpleasantly. Hitherto, those who had joined them had done so after the various parties had become acquainted, and then by unanimous vote they were assigned their task. This seemed another indication of the ironclad authority England intended to maintain over mission affairs. Consequently, Carey wrote Ryland, saying:

"I have scarcely ever written under such distress of mind. We are yours to live and die for you, but as your brothers, not as your servants. I beseech you, therefore, not to attempt to exercise a power over us to which we shall never submit . . . My heart is exceedingly wounded at the Society's proposal of the eight British trustees, and at several concomitant symptoms."

He goes on to point out that the money sent by the Home Society, even that raised to repair the loss by the fire, altogether about $150,000.00, was only enough to pay the

salaries of the European workers, had they taken salaries.
The money for native preachers, schools, lands, buildings,
both at Serampore and at various mission stations established elsewhere, for printing plants, paper mills, type
foundries, and all other such obligatory necessities had been
supplied by the missionaries themselves. In conclusion he
affirmed:

"The premises belong to the Society. We have made the
Society a present of them. But if the Society insists on the
measure proposed, we will, much as we are attached to the
place, evacuate it and purchase other premises, which while
given to God will not be given to the Society, and there we
will carry on our work, subject to no control but His most
Holy Word. In this we are of one mind, and here we shall
make our stand.

"We have always thought ourselves masters of the funds
produced by our own toil. We devote the whole to the
cause of God, and wish to do so to our dying day. But the
funds we produce, though devoted to the same object,
have never been so merged into the Society's funds as to
put them under others' control. We are your brothers, not
your hired servants. We have always accounted it our glory
to be related to the Society, and with them pursue the same
grand purpose, and we shall rejoice therein, so long as you
permit us; but we shall come under the power of none. I
do hope that the ideas of domination which Fuller never
thought of, but which the Society has imbibed since his
death, will be given up, as we shall never 'give place by
way of subjection, no, not for an hour.' "

Finally, however, goodwill and Christian courtesy ironed
out these difficulties. In 1820 a reconciliation was affected
with the dissatisfied band that had gone to Calcutta. Carey
wrote to his son Jabez, August 15, 1820:

"I am sure it will give you pleasure to hear that our
long continued dispute with the younger brethren in Calcutta

is now settled. We met together for this purpose some three weeks ago, and after each side gave up some trifling ideas and expressions, came to a reconciliation which I pray God may be lasting."

It took longer to smooth out the differences with the Home Society. In hope of bringing about peace both the Marshmans and Ward returned to England on furlough, thinking personal contact and explanations might produce a better understanding. This undoubtedly helped, but it was not until 1830 that the matter was adjusted satisfactorily. An actual transfer of the Serampore property was then made to the trustees in England, with the understanding that the original missionaries should occupy them without rent during their lifetime.

The grim reaper was busy with the little group. In 1820 Carey's second wife died. Although a frail invalid, she was a helpful, sympathetic companion and her death was a tremendous loss. Daily he had carried her during the last months down to her garden chair that she might enjoy the fragrance and glorious bloom about her. She was loved by all at the Mission. Carey cried out at her passing, saying, "My loss is irreparable! I am exceedingly lonely." To Dr. Ryland, he wrote:

"I am now called in Divine Providence to be a mourner again, having lately experienced the greatest domestic loss that a man can sustain. My dear wife was removed from me by death on Wednesday morning, May 30, about twenty minutes after midnight. She was about two months above sixty years old. We had been married thirteen years and three weeks, during all which season, I believe we had as great a share of conjugal happiness as ever was enjoyed by mortals. She was eminently pious and lived very near to God. The Bible was her daily delight, and next to God she lived only for me.

"It was her constant habit to compare every verse she

read in the various German, French, Italian and English versions, and never to pass by a difficulty till it was cleared up. In this respect she was of eminent use to me in the translation of the Word of God . . .

"My loss is irreparable, but still I dare not but perfectly acquiesce in the Divine will. So many merciful circumstances attend this very heavy affliction that still yield me support beyond anything I ever felt in other trials. I have no domestic strife on which to reflect and to add bitterness to my affliction . . . She was ready to depart."

The Marshmans' eldest daughter was the next death in the community. Then in August, 1822, their first Christian convert, Krishna Pal, was taken from them by cholera. He had been a faithful servant of the Master through afflictions and strifes and had planted and watered the vineyard of the Gospel in many humble sections of the country.

A second great blow came to Carey with the death of his son, Felix, in 1822. After he had regained his sanity, he had again become of invaluable assistance to his father, especially as a linguist. He was acknowledged "the completest Bengali linguist among India's Europeans." But the greatest of all blows to the Mission came with the death of Ward from cholera on March 7, 1823. He seemed intuitively to have gained the ability to enter the Indian mind, and was unmatched as a counselor to the native converts. He was regarded by some as "the best preacher at Serampore." Dr. Carey wrote concerning this loss:

"What a breech! Who can fill it? We hope in God. We need your prayers."

Ward had come to India as a consecrated printer, and without his assistance — managing the presses and supervising the printing of various translations and additions of the Bible — the work of William Carey would have been impossible. God had raised up this laborer and when he passed away only the heavenly Father could fill the void. Carey recognized that providing a worker to step into Ward's shoes must be a work of God.

It seemed as if the Mission were to be dogged by misfortune. While returning from Calcutta late one night on October 8, 1823, Carey slipped on the landing dock and was seriously injured. Inflamation, fever and abscesses were so severe it seemed he would not recover. Finally, however, he pulled through, though he could not lift his foot from the ground for two months, and it was as late as February before he could limp about the premises. William Carey, indomitable spirit that he was, insisted upon being carried to his classes in Calcutta, and to his preaching engagements in Serampore. Fortunately he was helped through these sufferings by the gentle ministrations of his third wife, Grace Hughes, whom he had recently married. He wrote Jabez:

"Her constant unremitting care and excellent nursing took off much of the weight of my illness."

Disaster followed close upon the heels of disaster. The Hoogly River overflowed and damaged Carey's house so badly that he had to be moved from the building. Likewise it wrought havoc in several of the school buildings and to the grounds, and made many in the town destitute. No financial help arrived from England, and in spite of Carey's illness he took on extra duties to earn funds to assist those in need.

In England, likewise, friends were passive. God was calling his humble servants to their eternal home. In 1816 Carey's father died. Then Dr. Ryland went to his heavenly reward. He was the last of the trio who had fulfilled their obligation and vow "to hold the ropes."

"It appears as if everything dear to me in England has now been removed," Carey wrote of this bereavement. "When I look I now see a blank. Were I to visit that dear country I should have an entirely new set of friendships to form."

Financial calamity descended upon the missionaries from 1830 to 1833, the year of Carey's death. One after another of the great business houses of Calcutta failed. The first went in January of 1830, with a loss of from three to five million pounds sterling, plunging thousands into ruin.

Parents of children in the Serampore schools were unable to pay for their tuition, so these institutions were seriously affected. Other financial crashes followed in 1832 and 1833, until Calcutta and the neighboring districts were in a panic. In May of 1833, when, as Carey said, "the earth was iron, the heavens brass, the rains but powder and dust," a terrific gale swept Bengal destroying or injuring almost every village on the river, strewing the shore with bodies of the dead and wreckage of the homes.

The beautiful mahogany trees in Carey's garden were uprooted, his conservatory wrecked and all his careful plantings of twenty years destroyed. Starvation faced the people. The drinking water was infected and the possibility of a serious cholera and plague epidemic grew. In face of these disasters the funds from the Mission dwindled. The first income to fail was Carey's salary as professor at Fort William College. The institution became simply an examining body. Owing to his long and valuable service Dr. Carey was given a pension, but it was only half of his former salary. At the same time his translation work for the government was suspended, further reducing his income, for Carey had received considerable money from this revenue.

These were sad blows to the now-aging workers. They were "dissolved in tears," as one of their associates said, and Marshman "could not find words for his feelings."

Carey had gone through hardships and near-starvation in Calcutta. He had suffered severe attacks of fever in the early swamps where he labored. He had many times faced official intolerance, and during the sixteen years of persecution by his English brethren he had been greatly abased. Even Fuller's death and that of his father had fallen heavily upon him. But the severest trial that the father of modern missions had been forced to endure were those three years from 1830 to 1833.

Carey wrote of this period, saying:

"I confess that the prospect of this great reduction of my salary lay very heavily on my mind at first, particularly as it would put out of my power the support of our missionary stations. I am, however, convinced of God's infinite wisdom and have implored Him to bend my mind to His will . . . It is His wont to make us realize our complete dependence upon Him."

Said Marshman:

"Carey can contribute little to the stations out of his pension, after he has supported his sister Mary, his late wife's eldest sister in France, and an orphan whom he has sent home to be educated in England, the expense of whose board, education and clothing lies wholly upon him; not to mention the expense of his own family . . . You ask, perhaps, how we expect to carry forward . . . I answer, through Divine aid."

William Carey had but one source of supply, and that was his heavenly Father. He was no stranger to dire extremities. He was a man who had built firmly upon the Rock of Righteousness. He was content as long as he knew he was in the center of God's will. He could not be blown by winds of discouragement, uprooted by the storms of criticism, nor discouraged by untoward circumstances, however great they might be. His mind was fixed in God, and as long as the heaven was clear above him William Carey faced the future with dauntless courage.

An appeal was made to England and this crisis, like the

calamity of the previous fire, not only brought quick aid but aroused a more widespread interest in the work. Thus the tragedy became a blessing in disguise. In acknowledging the receipt of the money, Carey wrote:

"How shall we sufficiently praise God, who in our great extremity stirred up His people thus willingly to offer their substance for His cause. My heart is toward them all, but most I desire to reconsecrate myself to that God who has brought forth such wonders."

To his son Jabez, Carey wrote,

"I am always told to be fearful and unbelieving as respects supplies, and yet God has appeared beyond my most sanguine expectation."

As the financial failures continued, one of the members of the mission staff said in a letter to a friend:

"Dr. Carey has lost his last farthing. Mrs. Grace Carey's competency has all gone. Every farthing of money Marshman had is also gone. After three and thirty years' labor, of the tenth reserved for old age, nothing remains but the house in which he lives and two small houses in Barrackpore. Distress is now universal. We can obtain no more money now to pay the salaries of our brethren. What we shall do I know not. Were the day to arrive when we should be compelled to give up some of our stations, we should soon have to lay Dr. Carey in his grave."

But though the darkness was dense, the Missionaries' faith burned brightly. In the letters their courage shone forth.

"We must go forward," one wrote, "trusting to an all-wise God. We must rekindle the flame of love and the ardor of faith . . . We dare not faint. God will provide. How He will, we cannot tell. It would be shameful to distrust Him who has before so singularly helped us . . . He who is the same yesterday, today and forever, knows what He purposes. On Him we must wait whilst doing all within our own ability . . . We are heirs to riches which will never fail."

Once again the homeland, as well as friends of the Mission around the world, came to the rescue and gifts poured in until "thankfulness and praise rang from one end of the Mission to the other." A member of the Mission staff joyously wrote, September 18, 1833:

"We are now able to restore all former salaries . . . We need fear no more lack of means for our work. Our most distressing necessity is His Spirit to make all our toil effectual for the conversion of men . . . When we see the hearts of God's people thus at His command because He so inclines them to help us, why should we ever doubt Him any more? . . . We have not yet learned a proper importunity in respect to our spiritual necessities. His mercy in hearing us for the lesser things should goad us to pray for His Spirit."

In the midst of these distresses, seemingly as a foregleam of grace for the trials that were shortly to beset Dr. Carey, a great victory was won which rejoiced the veteran missionary's heart. On Tuesday, December 4, 1829, the burning of widows upon their husband's funeral pyres was abolished. For almost thirty years Dr. Carey had been fighting this evil. Ever since 1802, when he had gathered information for Lord Wellesley on the Hindu murder of babies, and then later on his own initiative, about the burning of widows on their husband's funeral pyres, Carey had never relaxed his efforts to have this cruel practice outlawed.

This practice was so firmly entrenched in Hindu life that it seemed impossible to make any headway against it. When Lord Bentick became Governor-General in 1828, however, he instituted a thorough investigation of the practice and finally carried, in the teeth of all opposition, a "regulation in council" to declare the rite illegal and criminal.

The edict reached Carey for translation into the Bengali,

early Sunday morning as he was preparing for his preaching service. Never did he take up a piece of translation with greater joy. He hastily arranged for someone to take his place in the pulpit and gave his Sabbath day to the task. It must be done with the utmost care, "every sentence and every phrase being weighed with the most anxious deliberation," he avowed. There must be nothing that could be seized upon by the Brahmin to cause delay or frustration.

William Carey, now reaching the twilight years, could look back upon his career with a sense of satisfaction because this one great evil was abolished. Carey had humbly climbed the ladder of renown from a lowly position as a cobbler in England, until now, an elderly and venerable missionary, he was acclaimed around the world as one of the Church's brightest sons, and one of the Empire's most talented members.

Chapter 9

"ON THY KIND ARMS I FALL"

THERE ARE THREE BASIC TENETS upon which William Carey founded his missionary enterprise. First was the preaching of the Gospel in the people's native tongue. Second and outstanding was the translation of the Bible into the languages of India and neighboring nations. Finally he recognized that he must teach the young, both Christian and non-Christian, in vernacular schools.

The first of these activities resulted in the founding of churches, the second in numerous translations and editions of the Bible, and the third, in the educational systems which Carey established — culminating in the Serampore College.

As he increased in age and reached the sunset period of his life, Carey took greater pleasure in the college than in any other activity. He recognized that the work of carrying the Gospel to India must be accomplished through trained nationals, rather than through imported foreign missionaries. To achieve this end, he devoted his intellectual guidance during the latter years of his life to the schools which he and his fellow-missionaries had established.

In time these educational procedures and institutions called for an established curriculum, which meant, in most cases, the preparation of study texts and other corresponding research materials, a task in which Carey and his fellow-missionaries gloried.

As Carey pondered the educational project he had

139

founded, he felt that the college must be non-sectarian.
His mind was broad enough to envision the future and to
appreciate the cultural values of the Indian people. It
is a striking testimony to the greatness of Carey and Marshman, when one considers the progress made in the intellectual advancement of India during the last century, that
the lines they so clearly marked as the basis for the Indian
Christian University are those which are accepted by today's
most progressive thought.

They saw that the instructions in the higher education
must not be confined to a mere Western curriculum. They
realized that it must open, even to the poorest and humblest
Indian, the Scriptures and classics in the country's own
languages. Carey perceived that upon native preachers and
teachers the weight of this work would ultimately rest. He
was determined that they should be fully prepared by the
college for this responsibility.

"Let no man be able to despise you," he constantly
reiterated when challenging the Christian Indians with the
task before them. "Master the Sanskrit with such thorough-
ness, and then add such knowledge of the Scriptures and
Western science that, stronger than your antagonists, you
may foil them with their own trusted weapons and capture
their spoil."

This "spoil" was conceived by Carey as the soul of
India. He had come to India not only to win converts, but
also to alter the social and religious environment. To Carey
the spoils of India were the transformed thought-life and
regenerated souls of the natives.

Though a Baptist, he recognized that in India the distinctions of sex and denomination should be ignored by a broad
Christian spirit. He said:

"In a country so destitute of all which elevates the mind,
and so dependent on us for both political freedom and
moral improvement, it is surely our duty to forget the

distinctions which divide society in England, and to make common cause for the promotion of its welfare. It will be time enough a hundred years hence, when the country is filled with knowledge, and truth has triumphed over error, to think of sects and parties. Every public institution aiming at India's betterment ought to be constructed on so broad a basis as to invite the aid of all denominations."

During the construction years of the college, roughly from 1818 through 1820, Carey was elated at the progress. He entered into it with enthusiasm, arranging the library and museum personally. He took pride in welcoming the students, and on his week-ends, when free from his Calcutta duties, he took part in the college activities. He was sixty years old when the work was finally completed. During the next seven years, until the charter was obtained from the King of Denmark in 1827, he watched over the rapid development and the high attainment of the school with justifiable pride.

From this time until his death, he marshaled all the combined forces of his previous years of experience and training toward the direct end of making this final contribution to India's future welfare his best. He believed that a successful college must open its doors to all students and nationalities. Hence the enrollees during these years included Brahmin, Moslems, Punjabis, Mahrattas, Khasis, Arakanese and Bengalis. There was no section of the nation, no groups of people, no social strata not represented in the student body.

In a short time various magazines began to flow from the institution's life and work, all of which helped introduce it to the natives. They aided in preparing the way for further social and religious reforms of the various evils that had held the people in bondage. One such practice that Carey valiantly fought was the crude treatment of lepers. He never remained idle in his combat of this evil until a

leper hospital was established in Calcutta where those suf-
ferers from the world's most dread disease could find
asylum and treatment.

As a boy in his native England Carey had loved plants,
bird-life and animals; finding an unfailing source of delight in them. Busy as he was in India with the pursuits so
alien to such natural, botanical and zoological matters,
he never lost interest in these subjects, devoting his spare
moments to these interests.

"I have always," he wrote Andrew Fuller many years
before, "had a strong turn for natural history, especially
for botany, and know of nothing better to relax the mind
after close application."

At one time it seemed that he might become the superin-
tendent of the Calcutta Botanical Gardens. But God had a
greater position for him in the stream of Indian life.
Instead, Dr. Roxburgh became the government botanist and
laid the foundation for the botanical advancement and clas-
sification of India. Carey corresponded with the doctor
through the long years of his life. When the missionary
was at Mudnabutty they exchanged botanical specimens.
Carey, after his trip to Bhutan, sent rare plant specimens
from there to the doctor, one of which Roxburgh named
Careya in the missionary's honor.

Six months after coming to Serampore Carey sent Roxburgh a list of four hundred and twenty-seven species of
plants that he was already growing in his garden, although
every moment of his time had been crowded with the
duties of starting and maintaining the Mission. He asked
Roxburgh for sixty-six other specimens, saying, "My desires are unbounding." He went on to tell the personal
care he gave certain precious plants. Besides, he wrote frequently and at length about other experiments to find the
most suitable for the local soil and climate.

In time Carey read papers on agriculture before the

Asiatic Society. He was one of the first in India to plead for forestation. It was through Carey's genius that Dr. Roxburgh's life's work was finished. When the botanist was unable to work through failing health, Carey edited and printed his *The Hortus Bengalensis,* which was a catalog of the plants of the East India Company's Botanical Gardens in Calcutta. After Dr. Roxburgh died, Carey published the *Botanists' Flora Indica,* which became and remained a standard botanical work on the subject.

As early as 1811 he wrote a paper on agriculture, and more especially on the cultivation of timber, which in time found its place in a volume of the *Asiatic Researches.* Ten years later he wrote in the *Missionary Herald,* saying:

"I bless God I am as healthy as I ever remember to have been. I have for some time back had much at heart the formation of an agricultural society in India. Some months ago I had a conversation with Lord Hastings on the subject. He encouraged me to make an attempt, in consequence of which I published a prospectus and circulated it throughout India. The result is that on the 14th of September an agricultural and horticultural society was formed which consists already of about fifty members."

Andrew Fuller tells us that the Baptist Missionary Society sprang from the fertile workings of Carey's mind, and from that same prolific source suddenly came the Agricultural and Horticultural Society of India. According to Dr. George Smith this formed the model of the Royal Agricultural Society of England. There is little telling to what high estate William Carey might have attained had he invested his talents solely in scientific experimentation. Had he devoted his activities to the study of natural research he doubtless would have stood as one of the world's most famous agriculturists, botanists or geologists. But William Carey had met the Master at Calvary, and could not remain content to labor in less significant fields than that which was concerned solely with the transformation of human life and character through redemption by Jesus Christ. Hence botanical, agricultural, and even geological studies remained avocational in his broad interests.

As a missionary, he studied the health conditions and the abject poverty (bordering on starvation) of the natives. He felt that something should be done to better the food production in this fertile land. He expressed his regret that:

". . . in one of the finest countries of the world, the state of agriculture and horticulture is so abject and degraded and the people's food so poor and their comforts so meagre. India seems to have almost everything to learn about the clearing of jungles, the tillage of wastes, the draining of marshes, the banking of river courses, the irrigation of large areas, the mixing of composts and of manures, the rotation of crops, the betterment of tools and of transport, the breeding of stocks, the culture of new vegetables and herbs, the planting of orchards, the budding, grafting and pruning of fruit trees and the forestation of timbers. Their only orchards are clumps of mangoes crowded together without judgment. The recent introduction of the potato and the strawberry suggests what might be done."

With the formation of the Agricultural Society, Carey served as secretary for some time. The work went forward slowly, but in time grafted fruit trees were introduced and experiments begun in the raising of coffee, cotton, tobacco, sugar cane and some cereals. The missionary was indefatigable in his suggestions for better methods of irrigation, fertilizers and the protection of seedings. In fact, all parts of the work came under his scrutinizing eye. Many of the agricultural products now so valuable to India were introduced by Carey.

Had he not been a missionary he would have no doubt

achieved honors in the horticulture field. An avenue of beautiful trees in Calcutta's Botanical Gardens is named for him. A marble bust of him stands in the home of the Agri-Horticultural Society in Calcutta. He was elected a member of the Horticultural Society of London, and also of the Geological Society of England.

For forty-one years Carey was spared to serve God in India. He outlived nearly all of those who were associated with him in the establishment of the mission, such as Fuller, Sutcliff and Ryland in the homeland, and Dr. Thomas, Ward and Chamberlain, and other fellow-workers in India. During his prolonged residence, which was un-broken by furlough to England, he experienced several serious attacks of illness. In 1823 he suffered a severe case of fever which brought him to the brink of the grave. From that illness he never fully recovered.

This necessitated a restriction on his manifold duties. Yet he merely concentrated his efforts and abilities upon certain pursuits with a diligent persistency that brought greater achievement than would otherwise have been pos-sible. His chief desire was to complete the last revision of his Bengali version of the Bible, and he reserved sufficient strength for the accomplishment of that task.

Repeated fever attacks, followed by attending compli-cations, seriously enfeebled his constitution. In 1831 he thought that he had finished his race. He published his last book in 1832. But God was not ready to retire him. In the spring of 1833 Carey's health had sufficiently improved so that Missionary Leechman, who had just arrived from England to serve as Carey's assistant, said:

"Our venerable Dr. Carey is in excellent health and takes his turns in all our public services. Forty years ago the first of this month he administered the Lord's Supper to the church at Liecester and started on the morrow to embark for India. Through this long period of honorable toil the Lord has mercifully preserved him, and at our missionary prayer meeting held on the first of this month he delivered an interesting address to encourage us to persevere in the work of the Lord. We have also a private monthly prayer meeting held in Dr. Carey's study which is to me a meeting of uncommon interest.

"At our last meeting Dr. Carey read part of the history of Gideon and commented with deep feeling on the encouragement which that history affords, that the cause of God can be carried on to victory and triumph by feeble and apparently insufficient means."

Friends suggested to Carey that he relax his extensive labors, thus to lengthen his invaluable life. But with inveterate hatred of inactivity, he would sit at his desk when his physical strength was altogether unequal to the tremendous surging mental energy that bounded within. Often he was compelled to labor almost entirely from his couch. Even when thus prostrated he would work with proof sheets of the various editions of the Bible for revision.

"My being able to write to you," he said in the spring of 1833, in his letters to his sisters in England, "is quite unexpected by me and I believe by everyone else, but it appears to be the will of God that I should continue a little longer. How much longer that may be, I leave entirely with Him, and can only say, 'all the days of my appointed time will I wait till my change comes.'

"I was two months or more ago reduced to such a state of weakness that it appeared as though my mind was extinguished, and my weakness of body and sense of deep fatigue and exhaustion were such that I could scarcely speak, and it appeared that death would be no more felt than the removing from one chair to another."

He went on to say that he was able to sit and to lie in bed, and now and then to "read a proof sheet of the Scriptures. I am too weak to walk alone but just across the house, nor can I stand even a few minutes without support. I have every comfort that kind friends can afford, and feel generally a tranquil mind. I trust the great point is settled and I am ready to depart, but when that time will be, I leave with God."

It was indeed a difficult struggle and a great battle that Carey could look back upon, yet it was with a sense of triumph that he recognized the blessings of God, as he sat in his beautiful garden, planning future work, interviewing his friends or enjoying their fellowship. In this garden his son Jonathan, now a Supreme Court attorney, said that his father enjoyed his most pleasant moments of secret meditation and devotion. His favorite walk, when he was able, was the avenue from his home which ran behind the college to the building that housed the printing press.

His interest in the garden remained to the last. As long as he was able he was taken in a chair to visit his beloved resort. When that enjoyment was no longer possible his head gardener was regularly summoned into his room to receive instruction. On one such occasion, in a moment of depression, Carey said, "When I am gone Brother Marshman will turn the cows into the garden." But Marshman who was present, instantly replied:

"Far be it from me. Though I have not your botanical tastes, I shall consider the preservation of the garden in which you have taken so much delight as a sacred duty."

During these final days of his life Dr. Carey was visited by friends and famed people from around the world. Into his garden or room came such leaders as the Governor-General of India, the Bishop of Calcutta, teachers, businessmen, professors and humble Christian natives.

One of the most welcome visitors was young Alexander Duff, recently come to Calcutta for the purpose of starting a college. He was eager for Dr. Carey's advice. Dr. George Smith says of Duff's first interview with Carey:

"With one exception the other missionaries discouraged Duff's conclusion — that Calcutta must be the scene of his principal efforts and that his method must be different from that of all his predecessors in India. He had left to the last the aged Carey, in order that he might lay his whole case before the man whose apostolic successor he was to be. Landing at the college that one sweltering July day of 1830, the still ruddy Highlander strode up the flight of steps that led to the finest modern building in Asia. Turning to the left he sought the study of Carey where the greatest of missionary scholars was still working for India. There he beheld what seemed to be a little yellow man in a white jacket of whom he had already often heard, totter up to him and with outstretched arms solemnly bless him.

"The result of the conference was a double blessing, for Carey could speak with the influence at once of a scholar who had created the best college in the country, and of a vernacularist who had preached to the people for nearly half a century. The young Scotsman left his presence with the approval of the one authority whose opinion was best worth having."

When Missionary Duff visited Carey for the last time the two spent their moments in reviewing Carey's long and famed missionary life since Duff was mainly interested in that. His praise of Carey's work went on until finally the dying man whispered, "Pray." Duff knelt by the couch and prayed, and then arose to say his last goodbyes. As he passed from the room he thought he heard a feeble voice pronouncing his name. He turned to find the aged missionary calling him again to his side. He stepped back to the couch, and in a solemn, gracious, barely audible voice William Carey said:

"Mr. Duff, you have been speaking about Dr. Carey, Dr. Carey. When I am gone say nothing about Dr. Carey — speak about Dr. Carey's *Saviour*."

Duff went away rebuked and awed, with a solemn lesson in humility and spiritual evangelism burning in his heart that he could never forget.

George Gogerly, a contemporary, visited the veteran missionary just before his death, and of that visit he said:

"He was seated near his desk in the study, dressed in his usual neat attire. His eyes were closed and his hands clasped together. On his desk was the proof-sheet of the last chapter of the Bengali New Testament which he had revised a few days before. His appearance, as he sat there, with his few white locks and his placid, colorless face, filled me with a kind of awe, for he seemed as one listening to his Master's summons, and ready to go. I sat there for about half an hour without a word, for I feared to break that silence, and to call back to earth the spirit that seemed almost in heaven. At last, however, I spoke, and well do I remember the very words that passed between us."

"Dear friend," said Gogerly, "you seem to be standing on the very border of eternity. Do not think it wrong then that I ask your thoughts and feelings."

The question roused Dr. Carey. Slowly he opened his eyes, and then with a feeble though earnest voice he answered:

"I know in whom I have believed, and am persuaded that He is able to keep that which I have committed unto Him against that day. But when I think I am about to appear in God's holy presence, and I remember all my sins, I tremble."

Carey the veteran, who had proclaimed the redeeming Gospel of Christ for these many years in India, could say no more. Tears trickled down his cheeks and he lapsed back into the silence from which the visitor had aroused him.

On June 7, 1834, Missionaries Marshman and Mack visited with the doctor, and Mr. Mack wrote to a friend in England:

"Respecting the great days before Carey, a single shade of an anxiety has not crossed his mind ever since the be-beginning of his decay, so far as I am aware. His Christian experience partakes of that guileless integrity that has been the grand characteristic of his whole life. Often, when he was yet able to converse, has he said to his friends, 'I am sure that Christ will save all that come unto Him, and if I know anything of myself I think I know that I have come to Him.'"

Mack went on to say that the ascertaining of that all-important fact had been the object of Carey's recent honest self-examination, and the result was a "peaceful assurance that his hopes were well-grounded."

Having brought the inquiry to this happy conclusion, in the prospect of death Carey was enabled to "dismiss all further anxiety on the subject from his mind, and had committed all that concerned his life and death to the gracious care of God in perfect resignation to His will."

"We wonder much that he is yet alive," Mack concluded in his letter, "and should not be surprised were he to be taken off within an hour, nor could such an occurrence be regretted. It would only be weakness in us to wish to retain him. He is ripe for glory, and already dead to all that belongs to life."

Two days later, on June 9, 1834, at the age of 72, William Carey, son of God, famed missionary of India, humble servant of the nations, passed away in a tranquil manner to be with his Master. Near his couch was a picture of a beautiful shrub, that his eyes until the very last might rest upon that which gave him so much delight. A young missionary by the name of Leechman said of this passing:

"The last chord that vibrated in his heart was gratitude to God and to his people."

At his funeral he was honored as an outstanding English-

man, a missionary of supreme worth, and a man who stood
as a peer of any man of his generation. The Danish flag
was flown at half-mast. The notables of India attended the
services, as well as the humble Hindus and Mohammedans
into whose very heart and life he had been enabled to
enter.

In his last will and testament he said:

"I direct that before every other thing all my lawful
debts be paid, that my funeral be as plain as possible, that
I may be buried by the side of my second wife, Charlotte
Emilia Carey, and that the following inscription, and
nothing more, may be cut on the stone which commemorates
her, either above or below as there may be room:

WILLIAM CAREY

Born August 17, 1761: Died —

"A wretched, poor and helpless worm,
On Thy kind arms I fall."

Famed societies the world around honored him with many
memorials. Religious groups, philanthropic organizations
and churches in memorial services testified to their high
estimate of his holy character and consecrated labors. The
Baptist Missionary Society, to which he had given birth,
said:

"Endowed with extraordinary talents for the acquisition
of foreign languages, he delighted to consecrate them to the
noble purpose of unfolding to the nations of the East the
Holy Scriptures in their own tongue, a department of
sacred labor in which it pleased God to honor him beyond
any predecessor or contemporary in the mission field. Nor
was Dr. Carey less eminent for the holiness of his personal
character. Throughout his life he adorned the Gospel of
God, his Saviour, by the spirituality of mind and uprightness of his conduct, and especially by the deep

and unaffected humility which proved how largely he had imbibed the spirit of his blessed Master."

John Foster, celebrated essayist, writing to Rev. John Faucet, summed up the Christian world's estimate of this humble servant of God by saying:

" . . . Dr. Carey is unquestionably the very foremost name of our times in the *whole Christian world*. What an entrance it has been into that other world!"

The measure of William Carey is to be found in this statement made by him during the heat of India's battle:

"I have rejoiced that God has given me this great favor 'to preach among the Gentiles the unsearchable riches of Christ.' I would not change my station for all the societies in England, much as I prize them. Nor indeed for all the wealth of the world. May I but be useful in laying the foundation of the Church of Christ in India. I desire no greater reward and can receive no higher honor."

Printed in the United States of America

WOMEN OF FAITH SERIES

Amy Carmichael
Corrie ten Boom
Florence Nightingale
Gladys Aylward
Isobel Kuhn
Mary Slessor

MEN OF FAITH SERIES

Borden of Yale
Brother Andrew
C. S. Lewis
Charles Finney
Charles Spurgeon
Eric Liddell
George Muller
Hudson Taylor
Jim Elliot
Jonathan Goforth
John Hyde
John Wesley
Martin Luther
Samuel Morris
Terry Waite
William Carey

John and Betty Stam